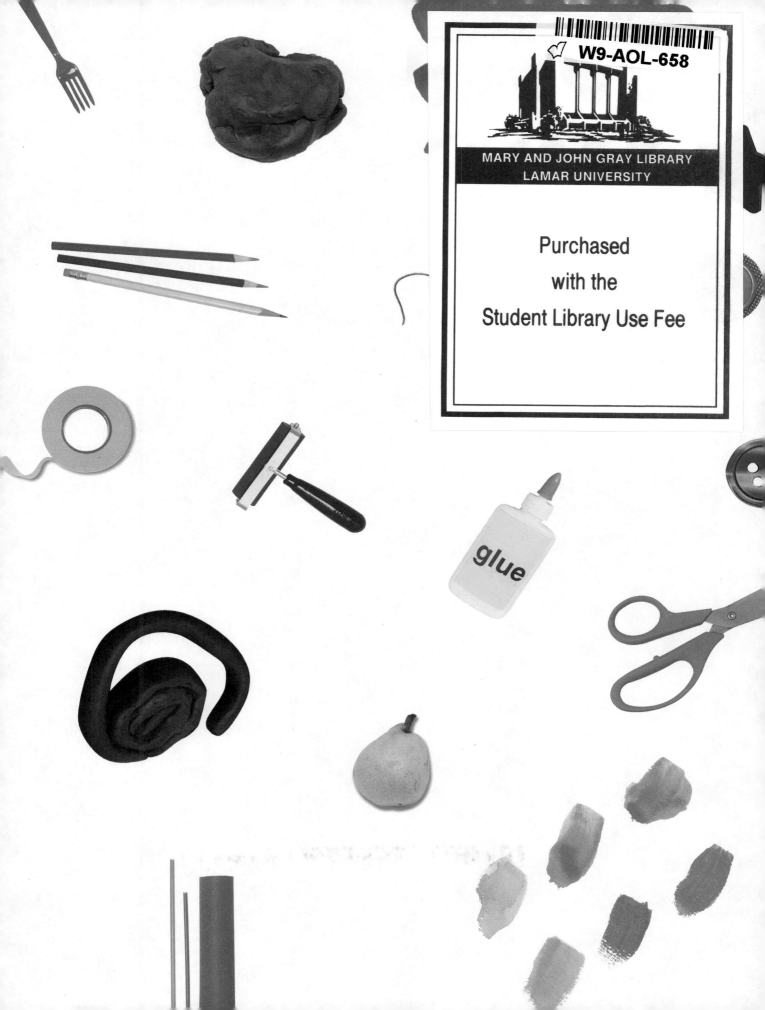

glue

ART Express

AUTHORS

Vesta A. H. Daniel

Lee Hanson

Kristen Pederson Marstaller

Susana R. Monteverde

Harcourt Brace & Company

Orlando   Atlanta   Austin   Boston   San Francisco   Chicago   Dallas   New York   Toronto   London

http://www.hbschool.com

Requests for permission to make copies of any part of the work should be mailed to: Permissions Department, Harcourt Brace & Company, 6277 Sea Harbor Drive, Orlando, Florida 32887-6777.

HARCOURT BRACE and Quill Design is a registered trademark of Harcourt Brace & Company. ART EXPRESS is a trademark of Harcourt Brace & Company.

Printed in the United States of America

ISBN 0-15-309315-3

3 4 5 6 7 8 9 0 048 2000 99 98

Dear Students,

What is art? How is it made? What makes it so special?

Artists use skill and imagination to make art. *Skill* is the ability to do something well. *Imagination* is the ability to dream up new ideas. When skill and imagination are put together, a piece of art is born!

In this book, you will find art from many cultures, made at many different times. You will learn why artists make art. You will also mix *your* skill and imagination as *you* make art — paintings, prints, sculptures, and more.

Are you ready to get started? Turn the page and let the art begin!

Sincerely,

The Authors

CONTENTS

UNIT 1 **Sharing Experiences** • 14

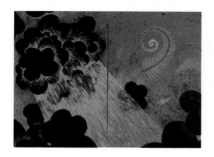

UNIT 2 # The Artist's Eye • 34

UNIT 3 Imagine a Story • 54

UNIT 4 **Artful Objects.** 74

 **Designs Old and New** • 94

Exploring Life's Riches ● 114

LOOKING AT ART

You may have seen art in books or museums. Do you remember some of the pieces better than others?

You may want to follow these steps and answer these questions when you look at a piece of art:

1 **Look closely** at the art. What do you see? Take some time to describe it.

2 **How do your eyes** move around the art? What part of it do you notice first? Think about why.

3 **Look at what** is happening in the art. What do you think the artist is trying to tell you?

4 **What do you think** of this piece of art? Discuss your thoughts with others.

Wherever you see art, take the time to really look at it.

KEEPING A
SKETCHBOOK

A **sketch** is a quick, simple drawing. Many artists draw sketches—and write notes about their artwork—in a **sketchbook**. Sketches are often redone many times.

Look at the photo of artist Chris Van Allsburg sketching. What do you think the first sketches of this finished painting from *The Wreck of the Zephyr* might have looked like?

These sketches and notes are from a student's sketchbook.

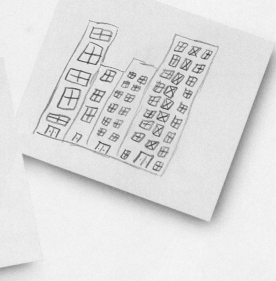

Ranger and me

Here are some ways to use your sketchbook:

- Plan your artworks.
- Record ideas for future projects.
- Write your thoughts about other people's art.
- Show what you see around you as an artist.

YOU, too, can keep an art sketchbook. Choose a notebook that is large enough to draw in. (Unlined paper works best.) Decorate the cover if you wish. Then start filling the pages with your ideas, notes, and drawings.

The Fiddler, Marc Chagall
1912–1913, Stedetiijk Museum, Amsterdam.

Sharing Experiences

How can a piece of art show an artist's feelings and memories?

Artists often share their memories and feelings through their art. When Marc Chagall painted *The Fiddler*, he brought to life someone he remembered from his childhood. The fiddler appears on a rooftop in a village—maybe the village where the artist grew up. If you painted a memory from your life, what would you show?

ABOUT MARC CHAGALL

Marc Chagall never forgot the small Russian village in which he grew up. His feelings and memories of his early life appear in nearly all of his artwork.

Creating with Lines

Why do you think artists chose to paint these scenes?

The artists who painted pictures **A** and **B** chose to paint places they knew well. Henri Matisse [ahn•REE ma•TEES] painted a corner of a room. How do you think he felt about this room?

Find **lines** in picture A that are thick, thin, curved, straight, broken, wavy, and zigzag. How would the painting be different if the artist had used only one or two kinds of lines?

A *The Window,* Henri Matisse
1916. Oil on canvas, 57 1/2 X 46 in.
The Detroit Institute of Arts, Detroit, MI.

Paul Klee [CLAY] painted a city park. Simple curved lines stand for the trees. What other objects do you see in picture B? What do you think the artist might say if he were telling you about this park?

B *Park near Lucerne,* **Paul Klee**
1938. Oil on newspaper mounted on burlap,
39 1/8 X 27 1/2 in. Klee Foundation,
Kunstmuseum, Bern, Switzerland.

IN THE STUDIO

MATERIALS

- colored markers
- white paper

Draw a place you know well.

Use markers to draw a picture of this place. Try to show how you feel about the place as you draw. How many kinds of lines can you use in your picture?

Shapes and Shadows

What do you think it would be like to live in one of these houses?

House by the Railroad,
Edward Hopper
1925. Oil on canvas, 24 X 29 in.
The Museum of Modern Art, New York.

American artists Edward Hopper and Charles Burchfield painted many pictures of houses and buildings they saw. They often gave their paintings a strong **mood**, or feeling.

What feeling do you get from each painting? Does the scene look lonely? Peaceful? Scary? Mysterious? Artists can use shadows to make certain **shapes** stand out. These shapes and shadows can help create a mysterious mood. What shapes do you see in picture **A**?

Look at the curving shapes of the trees in picture **B**. Would the house seem as mysterious without these shapes around it?

B ***Old House and Spruce Trees,*** **Charles Burchfield**
1951–1960. Watercolor on paper. 44 5/8 x 53 3/4 in. Archer M. Huntington Art Gallery, The University of Texas at Austin. 1951

IN THE STUDIO

MATERIALS

- **dark crayons or soft pencils**
- **white paper**

Draw a house or building. Make it look mysterious.

1. **Think of a house or building you would like to draw. Decide what else you might want in the picture. What time of day do you want to show?**

2. **Use soft pencils or dark crayons, or both, to draw your picture. Think of ways to create shadows to help give your picture a feeling of mystery.**

Chris Van Allsburg:
Painting an Adventure

How would you prove that you were the greatest sailor in the world? Would it be by braving a stormy ocean? Or would it be by doing something no sailor had ever done before, like sailing on air?

▼ **from *The Wreck of the Zephyr*, illustration by Chris Van Allsburg**

Chris Van Allsburg wrote and illustrated *The Wreck of the* Zephyr, a story about a boy who tries to prove *he* is the greatest sailor in the world. You can probably guess from these pictures that he had quite an adventure!

"I have a favorite kind of mood in my art," Chris Van Allsburg says. "I like things to be mysterious." How has he created a mood of mystery in his art?

from *The Wreck of the* Zephyr, illustration by Chris Van Allsburg

Chris Van Allsburg

WHAT DO **YOU** THINK ?

▶ **What would it be like to be in the boat in these pictures?**

▶ **Do you think these pictures would look more mysterious or less mysterious if they were in black and white? Why?**

Color and Feelings

How did the artists show that these rooms were special to them?

Room at Arles,
Vincent van Gogh
Van Gogh Museum, Amsterdam.

Vincent van Gogh [van GOH] and Gwen John both painted pictures of their own rooms. Which **colors** are bright and happy? Which are soft and quiet? How do you think Vincent van Gogh felt about his room? How did Gwen John feel about hers?

A Corner of the Artist's Room, Paris
Gwen John
Sheffield City Art Galleries.

Now look at the color wheel. Red, yellow, and blue are **primary colors**. Mixing two primary colors makes a **secondary color**. Find orange on the wheel. It is halfway between red and yellow. Red and yellow are primary colors that are mixed together to make the secondary color we call orange. Which two primary colors would you mix to make the secondary color green?

When you mix a primary color with a secondary color, you make an **intermediate color**. Find the intermediate colors on the color wheel.

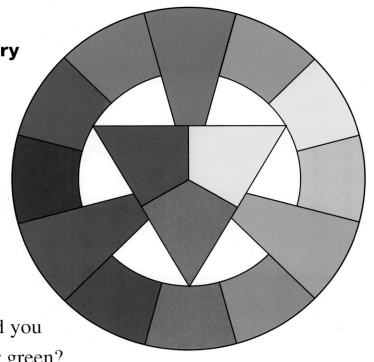

Color wheel

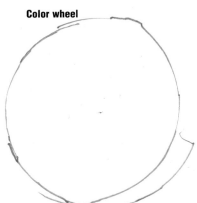

In the Studio

MATERIALS	Paint a picture of a room in your home.
• tempera paints • paintbrushes • white paper	Practice mixing colors to make the colors you need. Use the colors you have mixed in a way that shows your feelings about the room.

Color Choices

What is unusual about the colors you see in these pictures?

Pictures **A** and **B** show places that the artists remembered from their past. The artists changed some of the real colors to show their feelings.

Truong Thi Thinh [CHUNGK TEE TIN] came to the United States from Vietnam. What feeling about leaving her homeland does picture A express? How do you know?

Artists can also show feelings through **contrast**. One type of contrast is between **warm colors** and **cool colors**. We call reds, yellows, and oranges "warm colors" because they remind us of warm or hot things. Blues, greens, and purples are called "cool colors." What contrast between warm and cool colors do you see in picture A?

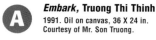

A *Embark,* **Truong Thi Thinh**
1991. Oil on canvas, 36 X 24 in.
Courtesy of Mr. Son Truong.

In picture B, Romare Bearden showed a house that his grandparents owned when he was a child. He used warm colors in the dining room. Where did he use cool colors? What kinds of memories do you think he had of staying with his grandparents?

IN THE STUDIO

MATERIALS

- tempera paints
- paintbrushes
- white paper

Paint a picture of a place you know.

Use some surprising colors or color contrasts to show how you feel about the place.

Interior Designer:
Creating a Mood with Color

What rooms in your house would you want bright and cheery?
What rooms would you want quiet and calm?

An interior designer is an artist who designs rooms and other indoor spaces. The designer chooses colors and objects to create a mood, or feeling, in a room.

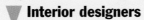
Interior designers

Color is probably the most important tool for an interior designer. Imagine yourself walking into each of these rooms. Do the rooms feel warm or cool? Lively or calm? Noisy or quiet? How do the colors create different moods in these two rooms?

WHAT DO **YOU** THINK ?

▶ If you could choose a new color for your room, what color would you choose? Why?

▶ Which of these two rooms would you rather spend time in? Why?

A Balanced Design

What experience does the artist share in this painting?

Artists may create a pleasing effect by placing objects in a picture in a certain way. The way the parts of a picture are arranged is called **balance**.

Draw an imaginary line down the middle of the picture. Compare the left and right sides of the picture. What do you notice? How did Mattie Lou O'Kelley balance the two sides of her painting?

This picture has **symmetrical balance**. The left and right sides of the lamp in the center are the same size and shape.

Reading Time, **Mattie Lou O'Kelley**
1981. Oil on canvas.

The objects on each side are placed the same way in relation to the midline.

Mattie Lou O'Kelley painted many scenes from her life in a small Georgia town. What feeling about past times does symmetrical balance help give this painting?

IN THE STUDIO

Use cut paper to make a picture with symmetrical balance.

1. Choose a symmetrical object for the center of your picture. Then decide on at least two people or objects to add to each side.

2. Cut the shapes of the objects from different kinds of paper.

3. Glue your shapes onto the large paper. Use crayons or markers to add details.

Window Views

How do you think these artists felt about the cities they painted?

Pictures **A** and **B** show views of large cities. The artists painted the views from inside their rooms.

Do the paintings show symmetrical balance? How do you know? Artists can also create balance when the two sides of a picture are not symmetrical. This kind of balance is called **asymmetrical**. The colorful window frame on the left side of picture A is balanced by the shapes and colors on the right side. The dark curtain on the left side of picture B is balanced by the shapes and lighter colors on the right side.

Would these two pictures be as interesting if the window frames had been centered on the outside scenes?

 Paris Through the Window,
Marc Chagall
1913. Oil on canvas, 53 1/2 x 55 3/4 in.
Guggenheim Museum, New York.

IN THE STUDIO

MATERIALS

- white paper
- colored markers
- tempera paints
- paintbrushes

Paint a window view with asymmetrical balance.

1. **Sketch an outside scene you might see through a window. Show the window frame and some of the objects inside the room. Place your window to one side of the picture.**

2. **Look at your sketch as you paint the window frame and the inside objects.**

3. **When the paint is dry, use colored markers to draw the scene outside the window.**

The artists in this unit have shared thoughts and feelings with you.

Some artists have shown you places that are important to them. Some have painted their memories. You have seen how artists use line, shape, and color to express feelings and create mood.

Bonjour, Monsieur Gauguin (Good Morning, Mr. Gauguin),
Paul Gauguin
1889. Oil on canvas, 36 1/2 X 29 in.
National Gallery, Prague.

What Did I Learn?

- **LOOK** at the painting on page 32. The artist, Paul Gauguin [goh•GAN], put himself in the picture. What contrast between warm and cool colors do you see? What feeling about the morning do the colors in the painting help show?

- **LOOK** back at the artworks in this unit. How many are paintings? Why do you think so many artists paint as a way to share their experiences?

- **FIND** the paintings in this unit that use symmetrical balance. Why do you think that symmetrical balance is not used as often in works of art?

- **THINK** about the artworks you created for this unit. Which piece has the strongest feeling or mood? How did you use line, color, and shape to help create the mood?

Guilin's Autumn, Wang Yani
1982.

The Artist's Eye

How do artists show that they see the world in different ways?

Every artist has his or her own way of looking at the world. Artists show their personal styles in different ways. Look at *Guilin's Autumn* on the left. Wang Yani has painted her feelings about this view of nature instead of its exact details. As you look at the art in this unit, think about how the artists see the world.

ABOUT WANG YANI

Wang Yani began painting pictures of animals when she was just three years old. As she grew older, she began painting the people and the world around her.

City Scenes

How did these artists show the time of day in their pictures?

A picture that shows a view of a city is called a **cityscape**. Mark Tobey and John Button observed scenes in New York City. Then they chose what they wanted to show in order to create a mood.

Broadway, **Mark Tobey**
1936. Tempera on masonite board,
26 X 19 1/4 in.
Metropolitan Museum of Art,
New York.

36

Mark Tobey used white lines to show the lively mood of a busy avenue. Start in a corner of picture **A** and trace a line with your finger. Feel how the line goes on and on, twisting and turning to form the shapes in the picture. Can you see tall buildings? Lights? Cars?

Picture **B** is a view of New York City at sunset. How did John Button contrast the buildings with the sky? How is the mood of this painting different from that of picture A?

Yellow Sunset, John Button
1963. Watercolor on paper, 8 in. x 12 in.
Fischbach Gallery, New York.

IN THE STUDIO

MATERIALS

- white paper
- yellow or other light-colored crayons
- watercolors
- paintbrush

Draw a view of a city at a certain time of day.

1. Use one or more light crayons to draw a cityscape on your paper. Draw as much as possible without lifting the crayon.

2. Choose one or more watercolors that will show the time of day. Brush a thin layer of watercolor over your drawing, and watch your cityscape appear.

Near and Far

 The Rocky Mountains, Albert Bierstadt
1863. Oil on canvas, 73 1/2 x 120 3/4 in.
The Metropolitan Museum of Art.

Which of these paintings is more like a photograph, and how?

Pictures **A** and **B** are both **landscapes**, outdoor scenes that show the beauty of nature.

Albert Bierstadt [BEER•stat] painted huge landscapes of the American West. What **details** can you see in the objects in picture A? Do the animals, people, rocks, and trees look lifelike? Why do you think Bierstadt put great detail in his scenes?

Emily Carr left out details in picture B. She was interested in expressing her feelings about nature, not in showing lifelike details.

Space is important in landscapes. Artists give the feeling of space by making some objects seem near and others seem far away. The part of the landscape nearest to you is called the **foreground**. In the foreground of picture A, you can see people, horses, and trees. The high mountains against the sky are in the **background**. What do you see in the foreground and background of picture B?

B *Mountain Forest,* **Emily Carr**
The Vancouver Art Gallery,
Vancouver, British Columbia.

IN THE STUDIO

MATERIALS

- **paper**
- **tempera paints**
- **paintbrushes**

Paint a landscape showing objects near and far away.

What objects will you show in the foreground and background? What mood do you want to create?

Choose several main colors to use in your landscape.

Valley Curtain

Instead of painting a landscape, these artists decided to change one!

The orange curtain in these pictures was an actual work of art in Rifle, Colorado. It was created by artists named Christo and Jeanne-Claude. To get an idea of the curtain's size, look below at the size of the people standing near it.

▲ **Jeanne-Claude and Christo**

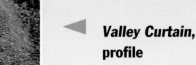

◀ *Valley Curtain, profile*

 *Valley Curtain, 1970–1971*

How do you think the artists got the idea to
stretch a giant curtain between two mountains?
What other ideas can you think of for changing
landscapes?

WHAT DO YOU THINK?

▶ **Suppose Christo and Jeanne-Claude put a piece
of art in your community. Where would it look
best?**

▶ **Look at the colors of the sky and ground. Why
do you think the artists chose an orange curtain?**

Water Scenes

What kind of weather do the colors in each painting seem to show?

Pleine Mer, **Eugene Boudin**
Christie's, London

*Green Sea Rocks and Boat,
Cape Split, Maine*, **John Marin**
1940. Watercolor on paper, 15 3/16 in. x
20 5/8 in. Archer M. Huntington Art Gallery,
University of Texas at Austin, TX

A **seascape** is a picture of an ocean or sea. It may also include the beach or shore.

Picture **A** is a seascape painted with oil paints. Can you imagine you are on a boat looking at the scene? Notice that some parts of the water are darker than others. This difference in color makes the water seem to be moving. The lightness or darkness of a color is its **value**.

Picture **B** is a seascape painted with watercolors.

Look at the blue used for the rocks and the shore. Where does its value change from light to dark? The colors of the water also go from dark to light. Where do the colors of the water end? Can you see a line of white foam crashing against the rocks?

Painters can make a **shade** of a color by adding black. With most kinds of paints, they make a **tint** of a color by adding white. With watercolors, they can make a color lighter by adding water.

IN THE STUDIO

MATERIALS

- **white paper**
- **watercolors**
- **paintbrushes**

Paint a seascape with watercolors.

1. **Imagine yourself standing on a beach or shore, looking out at the sea. What is the weather like? What do you see? Make a practice sketch.**

2. **Choose colors for the sky, the water, and the beach or shore. As you paint these parts of the scene, change the value of at least one of the colors. Let the paint dry.**

3. **When the paint is dry, go back and add details to your picture.**

Shapes in Nature

How did these artists show the beauty of nature through lines and shapes?

Artists often observe shapes in nature and use those shapes to create their own designs. Look at the way the artist used natural shapes in picture **A**. How are shapes in nature different from shapes in human-made objects such as buildings?

Compare the rabbit in picture **B** with those in picture **C**. How are the shapes the artists used the same? How are they different?

A **print** is made by covering an object or printing block with ink or paint and pressing paper onto it. Pictures B and C are both prints. They are made in different ways.

Flowering Evening Glory Vine,
Ogata Kenzan
Edo period. Hanging scroll; ink, colors, and gold on paper, 24 X 30 cm. William Sturgis Bigelow Collection. Museum of Fine Arts, Boston.

Helen Rabbit Baldwin, Melanie Yazzie
1995. Monotype, 10 X 14 in.

Rabbits, Henri-Charles Guérard
1893. Woodcut, 12 7/8 X 9 1/4 in.
Museum of Fine Arts, Boston.

IN THE STUDIO

MATERIALS

- plastic foam printing plate
- printing ink
- brayer
- white paper

Make a print that uses shapes from nature.

1. **Plan a picture based on shapes in nature. Draw the picture in pencil on a plastic foam printing plate.**

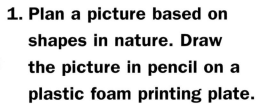

2. **Use a brayer to roll printing ink onto your plate.**

3. **Lay the paper on the inked surface. Press the paper gently with your fingertips, using a circular motion. You may want to use your print to make a greeting card.**

John Schoenherr

DRAWING ON REAL LIFE

What do you think this owl is about to do? How can you tell? Artists who choose to draw animals and natural objects in a realistic way pay very close attention to the details in their subjects. They want their pictures to look as real as possible.

▼ **from *Owl Moon*, illustration by John Schoenherr**

These pictures can be found in the book *Owl Moon* by Jane Yolen. The story is about a girl and her father who take a walk in the woods late at night. They are hoping to hear the call of an owl.

John Schoenherr drew

the pictures in *Owl Moon*. He spent a lot of time watching the owls in his backyard. He wanted to make sure that his pictures looked exciting and real.

John Schoenherr's illustrations were so good that he was awarded the Caldecott Medal. It is the highest award a children's book illustrator can receive.

from *Owl Moon*, illustration by John Schoenherr

John Schoenherr

WHAT DO **YOU** THINK ?

▶ **What kinds of animals or objects from nature do you like to draw?**

▶ **Do you think it would be easier to draw an animal from a photograph or from real life? Why?**

Nature in Motion

Hurricane, Bahamas, **Winslow Homer**
1898. Watercolor, 14 1/2 X 21 1/8 in.
The Metropolitan Museum of Art.

How does each artist show the power of a storm?

Look at the objects each artist used to show a storm. Winslow Homer used trees and clouds in picture **A**. These are objects you might expect in a storm scene. What is different about the way Louisa Chase combined objects in picture **B**?

Chase used **diagonal**, or slanting, lines for the rain. Why do you think she painted the rain this way? She used graceful, curved lines to paint the leaf and the hand. What feeling about the rain do these curved lines help show?

What kinds of lines do you see in picture A? Which lines help show motion?

IN THE STUDIO

MATERIALS

- **oaktag or cardboard**
- **foil**
- **tissue paper and other papers**
- **glue**
- **scissors**
- **markers or crayons**

Create a weather scene with cut and torn paper.

1. **Think of an exciting weather scene. How can you show nature in motion?**

2. **Cut or tear tissue paper, foil, or other paper to make the objects for your scene.**

3. **Arrange the paper pieces on oaktag or cardboard, and glue them down. If you wish, add details with markers or crayons.**

Fantastic Environments

How do you think these artists got the ideas for their pictures?

Two artists worked together to paint the natural environment in picture **A**. They studied the ocean environment and then used their imaginations to paint the scene. Can you tell what part of the scene each painted?

A *Dolphin Moon*, **Wyland and Tabora**
1991. Oil, 48 in. round.

Picture **B** shows animals in their arctic environment. What parts of the painting look real to you? What parts look like fantasy? How does this touch of fantasy help celebrate the wonders of nature?

B

Northern Lights, Melissa Miller
1982. Oil on canvas, 66 in. X 74 in.

IN THE STUDIO

MATERIALS

- shoe box and lid
- tempera paints
- paintbrushes
- markers
- tissue paper
- scissors
- glue
- tape
- twigs, grass, hay, or other natural materials

Create a diorama showing a natural environment. Add an animal to the scene.

1. With a partner, plan a diorama of an outdoor scene. Will you show a real-life scene or a fantasy? Will you combine the two?

2. Cut out one of the long sides of the shoe box. Paint your outdoor scene on the sides and bottom of the box. Add natural materials to your scene.

3. Trade boxes with another pair of students. With your partner, think of an animal to make for their diorama. Draw the animal on the shoe box lid, and cut it out. Then glue it into the diorama.

If you look at the world with an artist's eye, you can find ideas for art everywhere.

In this unit, you have seen how artists respond to human-made and natural environments. Artists combine what they see and what they imagine to create exciting new artworks.

Landscape with Cows and Camel,
August Macke
1914. Oil on canvas,
47 X 54 cm. Kunsthaus, Zurich.

What Did I Learn?

- **CHOOSE** a scene you like from the artworks you created for this unit. Tell what it shows or communicates that a photograph of the scene would not.

- **FIND** the scenes in Lesson 9, 11, and 12 that have a foreground and a background to show distance.

- **EXPLAIN** how August Macke used both what he saw and what he imagined to create the picture on page 52.

- **TELL** what natural shapes and what human-made shapes you see in *Landscape with Cows and Camel*. Find another artwork in this unit that uses both natural and human-made shapes. Compare the artists' use of shapes in the two pictures.

Self-Portrait, Jacob Lawrence
1977. Gouache on paper, 23 X 31 in.
Collection of the National Academy of Design, New York.

Imagine a Story

Artists may tell stories through their artwork. They may tell us about themselves, about others, or about special events. Jacob Lawrence created this painting of himself by looking in a mirror. He told something about himself by the objects he chose to paint in the background. If you painted a picture of yourself, what story would you tell? How would you tell it?

How can

a picture

tell a story?

ABOUT JACOB LAWRENCE

Most of Jacob Lawrence's paintings show the culture and lives of African Americans. People enjoy his colorful style and powerful stories.

Looking at Ourselves

What are these artists telling about themselves in these pictures?

A **self-portrait** shows the artist who created it. Do you think artists create self-portraits just to show what they look like? What other reasons might they have?

When you look at picture **A**, what do you see first—the artist's face or his foot? David Hockney

created this self-portrait by cutting up photographs and putting the pieces together. What do you notice about the sizes of the pieces? **Proportion** is the size of one thing compared to the size of another. Why do you think Hockney changed the proportion of his body in this picture?

In picture **B**, GG Kopilak painted her reflection in an iron. What does she show herself doing in her self-portrait? She did not put herself in the center of the picture or make herself very large. How does she draw your attention to her reflection?

 Self-Portrait with Folded Legs, L.A., Sept. 1982,
David Hockney
1982. Photo collage, 24 1/2 x 11 3/4 in.

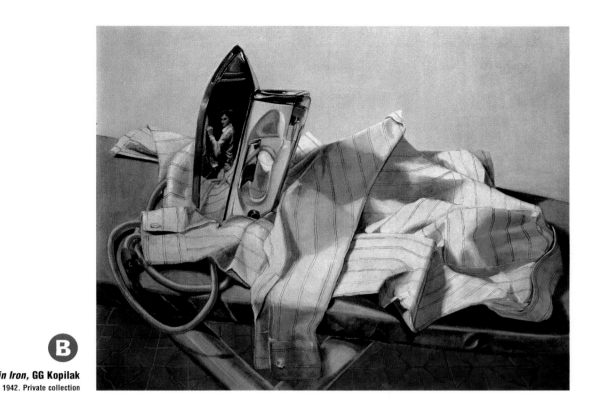

B

Self Portrait in Iron, GG Kopilak
1942. Private collection

IN THE STUDIO

MATERIALS

- mirror or other reflecting object
- heavy paper or cardboard
- tempera paints
- paintbrushes
- paper plate for mixing colors

Paint a self-portrait.

1. Look at yourself in a mirror or other reflecting object. In your sketchbook, sketch ideas for a self-portrait. What do you want to tell about yourself? What else can you put into the picture to add interest to your self-portrait?

2. Paint your self-portrait on paper or cardboard. Let the paint dry. Then paint other details on your self-portrait.

57

Looking at Others

How did these artists tell something about the people they painted?

A **portrait** is a work of art that shows a person or several people.

In most portraits the person is shown from the front. In picture **A**, however, Mary Cassatt shows the woman from behind. Does the woman seem to know someone is watching her? What might she be thinking?

***The Lamp,* Mary Cassatt**
1891. Worcester Art Museum, Worcester, MA

In picture **B** the girl is shown from the side. How would this portrait be different if the girl were shown from the front? How does Palmer Hayden use color and detail to help tell about the girl?

B *Mother Goose Tales,* **Palmer Hayden** Oil, 22 1/2 X 25 3/4 in.

IN THE STUDIO

MATERIALS

- drawing paper
- oil pastels

Draw a portrait of a model.

Sketch the model from an angle other than the front. Use oil pastels to add color and detail. How can you make your portrait tell a story?

PATRICIA POLACCO'S
SPECIAL MEMORIES

Did you know that a quilt can tell a family's story? Some families sew quilts from scraps of old clothing. The scraps and the patterns they make remind them of special times.

▼ from *The Keeping Quilt,*
illustration by Patricia Polacco

Patricia Polacco wrote and illustrated *The Keeping Quilt* based on her family's experiences and traditions. Her drawings show how her family quilt has been used over the years.

Think of special times that your family has had. What ways might you use to remember them and pass them on?

from *The Keeping Quilt*, illustrations by Patricia Polacco

WHAT DO YOU THINK ?

▶ **Why do you think Patricia Polacco drew only the quilt in color?**

▶ **If you made a family quilt, what special times would you show in it?**

Center of Interest

What do you think is about to happen in this picture?

This picture tells an exciting story, doesn't it? What action do you see? How does the artist show what is about to happen?

Many works of art have a **center of interest** that gets your attention. The center of interest may or may not be at the center of the artwork, but it

Wreck of the Ole '97, **Thomas Hart Benton**
1943. Oil and tempera on canvas mounted on panel, 29 1/4 X 46 in.
Hunter Museum of American Art, Chattanooga, Tennessee.

always stands out. An artist can create **emphasis**, or make part of the artwork stand out, in many ways.

Thomas Hart Benton leads your eye to the center of interest by the way he placed the objects in this painting. Start with the girl who is falling off the wagon. Follow the wagon as it rises toward the center of the painting. Then follow the train and track down the right side. Do you see the outline of a triangle pointing to the center of interest?

Now start with the fencepost at the bottom left. Can you find the outline of another triangle pointing to the center of interest?

IN THE STUDIO

MATERIALS

- **drawing paper**
- **oil pastels**

Draw an action scene from a favorite story.
Decide what the center of interest will be. How will it get the viewers' attention? Use oil pastels to draw the scene.

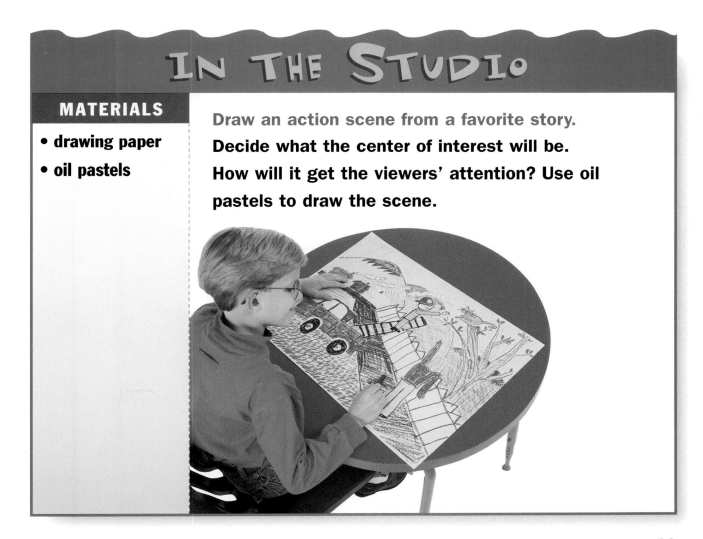

Celebrations

What shapes and colors are repeated in each picture?

Both of these paintings tell how people celebrate special times.

In picture **A** William Doriani shows a Flag Day parade. Look at how the marching figures, the flags, and the tree shapes are repeated. This repetition creates **visual rhythm**. Can you imagine the rhythm of the marching feet? Do you think the rhythm in this painting matches the rhythm of the feet?

In picture **B** Charles Searles shows African dancers wearing beautiful costumes. Notice the way the repeated shapes of the dancers create rhythm. Which dancers are wearing matching costumes?

 Flag Day, **William Doriani**
1935. Oil on canvas, 12 1/4 X 35 5/8 in.,
Museum of Modern Art, New York.

Dancer Series, Charles Searles
1975. Acrylic on canvas, 65 1/8 X 75 1/8 in.

The way the lines, shapes, and colors in the costumes are repeated is called **pattern**. What makes each dancer different from the others?

IN THE STUDIO

MATERIALS

- **drawing paper**
- **oil pastels**
- **fabric scraps**
- **scissors**
- **glue**

Create a picture that shows people dressed for a special occasion.

What are they celebrating? How are they moving? Use pattern and visual rhythm to create a lively mood.

CONNECTIONS CELEBRATION ART

Parade Costumes

Isn't it fun to watch a parade? Parades are held to celebrate all sorts of special occasions. What kinds of parades do you know about? Have you ever seen a parade in person or on TV?

▼ **The Battle of Flowers Parade, San Antonio, Texas**

Festive Brazilian parade.

Everywhere you see people in brightly colored costumes. Some costumes are shiny with sequins. Some people wear fantastic hats or headdresses. Some costumes have historical or traditional meanings. They all make a parade more exciting!

Decorated elephants, India, 1650

▶ **Which of the costumes in these pictures do you like best? Why?**

▶ **In what ways is designing a parade costume like painting a picture?**

Beyond Ourselves

What would you feel like doing if you wore one of these masks?

Tabwa Mask
Stanley Collection of African Art,
University of Iowa Museum of Art, Iowa City.

The masks in pictures **A** and **B** have lines, shapes, and colors that form patterns. Notice that each mask is symmetrical, like the human face.

In many cultures, masks have been used for thousands of years. Picture A shows a mask from central Africa. It is made from glass beads, feathers, animal skins, leather, and plants. How would the parts of the mask feel if you touched them? The way something feels is its **texture**. The different textures in the mask help make it interesting.

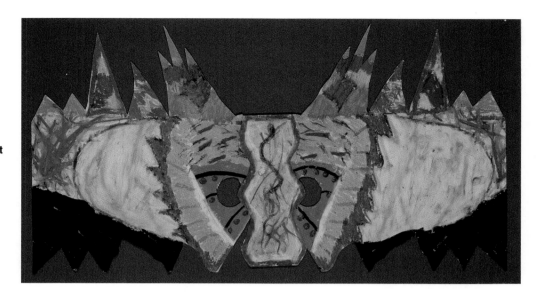

B Student art

IN THE STUDIO

MATERIALS

- cardboard or tagboard
- oil pastels
- scissors
- masking tape
- dowel or stick

Make a mask with a pattern. Match the proportions of your face.

1. Hold the tagboard in front of your face. Ask a partner to use a crayon to mark where your eyes and mouth are. Cut out the openings.

2. Use oil pastels to draw a pattern with repeating shapes and colors. Try blending colors, as the student artist did in picture B. If you wish, add other materials to decorate your mask.

3. Tape the dowel or stick to the back of your mask.

Performing Puppets

Why do people use puppets to tell stories?

Like masks, puppets are often used to tell stories. In fact, in many cultures, making masks led to making puppets. Look at picture **A**. Notice how the puppet's carved face looks like a mask. The North American Indians tied strings to puppets like this one to make them move.

The puppet in picture **B** is a hand puppet. The Swiss artist Paul Klee [KLAY] made this puppet for his son.

 Nishka marionette from Northwest Coast Indian cultures
National Museum of the American Indian

70

Klee got his idea for the puppet from Inuit, or Eskimo, art. How is it like the puppet in picture A?

Today puppets are used to entertain people all over the world. Puppet plays may tell traditional stories or new ones. Puppet artists use their imaginations to make their puppets works of art.

B **Eskimo puppet, Paul Klee**
1924. Wood, horseshoe, plaster.

IN THE STUDIO

MATERIALS

- **newspaper**
- **pulp papier-mâché**
- **masking tape**
- **cardboard tubes**
- **tempera paints**
- **paintbrushes**
- **fabric**
- **glue**
- **buttons, yarn, and other found objects**

Make a hand puppet from papier-mâché.

1. **Choose a story character for your puppet. To make its head, crumple newspaper into a ball and wrap it with tape. Then tape the head to the cardboard tube.**

2. **Mix the pulp papier-mâché with water. Cover the head and body with the pulp. Shape the puppet's face.**

3. **When the papier-mâché is dry, you can paint your puppet. Use fabric and other materials to make clothing and hair.**

Could you imagine a story as you looked at any of the pictures, masks, and puppets in this unit?

Through their artworks, artists often tell stories about themselves, about others, and about real and imaginary events. Visual stories entertain us. They also show the meaning of events.

The Mind at Play #10, Sharon Maczko
1987. Watercolor, 23 X 37 in.

What Did I Learn?

- **LOOK** at the paintings and drawings you made for this unit. Choose one that tells a story. How were you able to tell a story by showing only one moment in time?

- **FIND** the center of interest in the painting on page 72. Compare this painting with *Wreck of the Ole '97* in Lesson 15. How does each artist draw attention to the center of interest?

- **FIND** a painting in this unit that does not have a center of interest. Explain why the painting does not have or need a center of interest.

- **EXPLAIN** whether you think the masks and puppets in this unit are works of art.

glue

Three batik parasols, Inga Hunter
1977.

Artful Objects

How can

art make

everyday life

more fun?

Look around you and name some of the objects that you see every day. Are some objects more interesting than others? What makes them so? These umbrellas, also called parasols, were created by an artist. Have you ever used art to add beauty to an everyday object? What did you do?

ABOUT INGA HUNTER

Inga Hunter is an artist in Australia. She works with fabric, wax, and dye to create beautiful fabric prints called batiks.

Weavers at Work

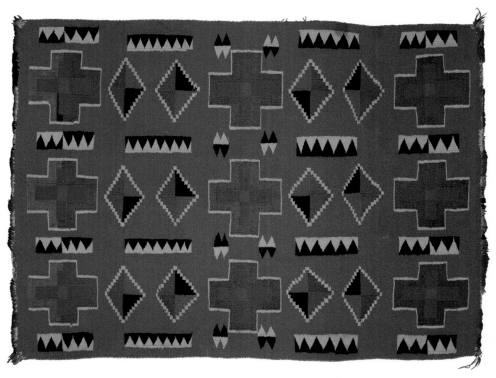

 Navajo transitional child's serapes
1880's. 34 X 45 in. Germantown.

Why did the artists take the time to make these objects so beautiful?

The object in picture **A** is a Navajo "wearing blanket." It was worn like a coat. A Navajo weaver made it both useful and beautiful. Picture **B** shows Navajo women making a **weaving**. The frame that holds the weaving is called a **loom**. What do you think the weaving will be used for?

Weavings are made from **fibers** such as thread or yarn. In picture B, look at the fibers running from the top to the bottom of the loom. They are called the **warp**. The fibers that go from side to side and form the pattern are called the **weft**.

Notice the different colors the women are using in picture B. They are creating an interesting pattern in their weaving. The pattern in picture A is called the Spider Woman Cross. Navajo myths say that Spider Woman taught the people to weave.

 Navajo Weavers, **Harrison Begay**
1948. 14 1/16 in. x 12 3/4 in. Watercolor.
Philbrook Museum of Art, Tulsa, OK.

IN THE STUDIO

MATERIALS

- piece of heavy cardboard
- masking tape
- colored string or yarn
- scissors

Make a loom. Use it to weave a wall hanging.

1. **Cut slits at the top and bottom of the cardboard.**

2. **Put yarn or string through the slits from top to bottom to make the warp. Tape both ends to the back.**

3. **Plan a design for your wall hanging. Weave the weft fiber over and under the warp to create your design. What colors will you use to create an interesting pattern?**

Patterns and Pictures

How are these pictures different from paintings?

Fireplace surround from the Patrick J. King House, **George Washington Maher** 1901. Oak, glass mosaic, and gold enamel. Los Angeles County Museum of Art.

Pictures **A** and **B** are examples of **mosaics**. A mosaic is a picture or design formed with small pieces of glass, tile, stone, colored paper, or other materials.

The mosaic in picture A was created for the fireplace of a house in Chicago. It is made from pieces of glass. Why do you think the artist used a symmetrical design?

The mosaic in picture B was created over 2,000 years ago. It was found in the city of Pompeii many years after the city was destroyed by a volcano. The people of Pompeii put mosaics on the walls of many houses and buildings. Picture B is called *Cave Canem*, which means "Beware of the dog." Where do you think this mosaic was put?

 Cave Canem
About 90 B.C. Mosaic found at Pompeii.
Museo Nazionale, Naples, Italy.

IN THE STUDIO

MATERIALS

- box with lid, such as a shoe box
- construction paper
- old magazines and catalogs
- scissors
- glue
- tempera paints
- paintbrushes

Decorate a box with cut paper to create a mosaic.

1. **Cut a piece of construction paper the same size as your box lid. Glue it to the lid.**

2. **Lightly draw a picture or design on it. Cut the paper and catalog pages into small pieces. Glue the pieces on your drawing to make your mosaic. Be sure to cover the entire lid.**

3. **Paint the sides of the box and the box lid.**

WHAT'S IN A MUSEUM?

When is a chair more than a chair?
When it is also a work of art!

You expect to see paintings
and sculptures in an art
museum. But you might be
surprised by some of the other
things you see. These pictures show
objects on display at the Museum
of Modern Art in New York City.

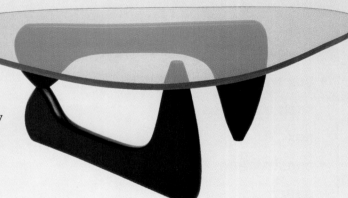

Table, **Isamu Noguchi**
1944. Ebonized birch and glass.
15 5/8 X 50 X 36 in. (39.7 X 127 X 91.4 cm).
Museum of Modern Art, New York.

Paimio Armchair, **Alvar Aalto**
1931–32. Birch plywood.
26 X 23 3/4 X 34 7/8 in. (66 X 60.5 X 88.5 cm).
Museum of Modern Art, New York.

Where do you usually see tables and chairs? Where have you seen tents before? Why do you think the objects shown here are in an art museum?

Red and Blue Chair, Gerrit Rietveld
About 1918. Painted wood.
34 1/8 X 26 1/2 X 26 1/2 in. (86.5 X 67.3 X 67.3 cm).
Museum of Modern Art, New York.

Tent. Charles W. Moss
1982. Nylon and aluminized nylon.
48 in. X 6 ft 8 in. X 7 ft 9 in.
(122 X 203.2 X 236.2 cm).
Museum of Modern Art, New York.

WHAT DO **YOU** THINK ?

▶ **Would you like to sit on these chairs, have this table in your home, or camp out in this tent? Why or why not?**

▶ **How are these objects different from similar objects that people use every day?**

Useful Forms

How did artists make these everyday objects interesting?

The Macaw Bowl in picture **A** has a bird's head for a handle. A macaw is a kind of parrot. Look at the way the artist decorated the bowl. How did the artist use a bird on the vase in picture **B**?

In picture **C**, the artist used the form of a pillow to create an unusual pitcher. A **form**, or three-dimensional shape, has height, length, and depth. The *Pillow Pitcher* is 16 inches high, 22 inches wide,

A

Macaw Bowl
ca. 1300A.D. Earthenware with polychrome slip, 5 1/8 X 14 1/2 in. Museum of Fine Arts, Houston.

and 12 inches deep (front to back). Do you think this pitcher would be useful for pouring liquids?

Some artists who work with clay to form objects use the **pinch** method. The artist pinches, pulls, and presses the clay by hand.

B **Vase with Handle in the Form of a Bird**
900–1250. Plumbate terra-cotta.

C *Pillow Pitcher*, Betty Woodman
1979. Earthenware, 16 X 22 X 12 in. Everson Museum of Art.

In The Studio

MATERIALS

- clay
- carving tools such as pencils and paper clips

Make a pinch pot from clay. Put something unusual in the rim, handle, or lid.

1. Use the pinch method to shape a pot or other container from clay. What can you add to your pot to make it special?

2. Use pencils or other objects to carve designs into your pot.

Uncommon Designs

How did artists show a sense of humor in these designs?

The objects in pictures **A** and **B** may not look much like chairs, but that is what they are. Pedro Friedeberg [FREED•berg] carved the chairs in picture A from wood. Alexander Calder used steel, wire, cloth, and painted paper to make the chair and lamp in picture B. Compare the designs of these chairs with those of the chairs you use every day.

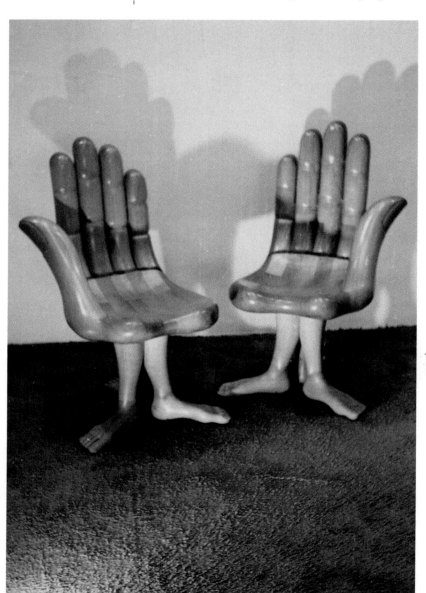

 **A** Two hand chairs, **Pedro Friedeberg** Hand-carved from wood, 3 feet.

Have you ever thought of a new design for an everyday object? Think about the furniture, cars, and household objects you see every day. Why do you think they are shaped the way they are? **Industrial designers** are artists who create interesting and pleasing forms for useful items. An industrial designer starts by sketching many views of an object. Then he or she builds a model of the object. The object may be one-of-a-kind or it may be mass-produced.

Elephant Chair with Lamp, **Alexander Calder**
1928. Galvanized sheet steel, iron wire, lead, cloth, and painted paper construction, 7 7/8 X 3 1/2 X 4 1/8 in. The Museum of Modern Art, New York.

IN THE STUDIO

MATERIALS

- **cardboard**
- **craft sticks**
- **toothpicks**
- **wire**
- **glue**
- **tape**

Create a model of a piece of furniture or other household object.

Decide what kind of object you want to design. Use your imagination. How can you create an object that is fun as well as useful? Use any materials you like to make your model.

IMAGINATIVE BICYCLES

Arthur and Christopher Dillon on the tricycle designed and built by Arthur Dillon

Take a bicycle and add your imagination. What new kind of bike could you design?

Look at the giant tricycle that Arthur Dillon and his son are riding. It is 11 feet high and 22 feet long. Arthur Dillon designed it and built it himself. What do you think riding it would be like?

The bike with no pedals is called a gravity bike. Dwight Garland III is riding it downhill. Do you suppose a gravity bike can go uphill?

What do you think of Greg de Alba's purple lowrider bike below? Many lowrider bikes have fancy paint jobs, bells, whistles, and funny sirens.

Greg de Alba and others on customized lowrider bicycles

WHAT DO **YOU** THINK ?

▶ **Which one of these bikes would you most like to own? Why?**

▶ **Why do you think someone would take the time to design a new kind of bicycle?**

Colorful Designs

Where do you think the artists got their ideas for these designs?

A **Blouse with palm nut tree**
Cloth mola.
Collection of Ann Parker and Avon Neal.

Pictures **A** and **B** are examples of **molas**. They were made by the Cuña people of Panama. A mola is a colorful design made of cloth. The mola in picture A has been sewn in a blouse.

Mola makers get ideas for their designs from the world around them. What familiar objects do you see in these mola patterns?

Molas are made by sewing together layers of different-colored cloth. The design is cut through the

layers so that the colors underneath can show through. Sometimes small cloth patches of other colors are stitched between the layers.

Look at the colors of the molas in pictures A and B. The Cuña people like bright colors. They usually use red or black for the top layer of their molas.

B *Tony the Tiger*
Cloth mola.
Collection of Ann Parker and Avon Neal.

IN THE STUDIO

MATERIALS

- **4 sheets of construction paper of different colors**
- **sheet of black construction paper**
- **glue**
- **scissors**

Make a mola from cut paper.

1. **Draw the outline of a familiar object on a piece of colored construction paper. Cut it out.**

2. **Glue the object onto paper of a different color. Draw a larger outline around the object. Cut it out. Repeat these steps until you have four layers.**

3. **Glue your mola onto a full sheet of black paper. Fill in the background with a design of colored paper scraps.**

Pictures on Cloth

 Tubular sarong, northern or western Java
Batik, Museum of Fine Arts, Boston.

Why do you think artists try different materials and ways of creating designs on fabrics?

The cloth designs in pictures **A** and **B** were created by a method called **batik** [bah•TEEK]. Part of the fabric is covered with wax. Then the fabric is dyed. The dye colors the fabric but does not stick to the wax. Then the wax is peeled off to show a design.

The batik in picture A is a sarong, a piece of cloth that wraps around the body. This sarong was created in Java, an island that is famous for its batiks.

90

Picture B is a page for the month of July from a calendar made by Russian children. Where was wax used in their design?

IN THE STUDIO

MATERIALS

- **piece of muslin**
- **white tempera paint**
- **acrylic paints**
- **paintbrushes**

Use tempera and acrylic paints to create a batik.

1. **Think about a design for the month of your birthday. Use the white tempera paint to draw the design on the muslin. Allow the paint to dry completely.**

2. **Mix acrylic paints with water to make them thin and runny. Brush paint over the whole piece of muslin to create your batik.**

3. **When the paint dries, dip your cloth in water. Rub off the white tempera paint.**

From earliest times, people have been creative in making the objects they use in their daily lives.

Many people still choose to make or decorate objects they use. In this unit, you have seen how artists have made some everyday objects especially beautiful or interesting.

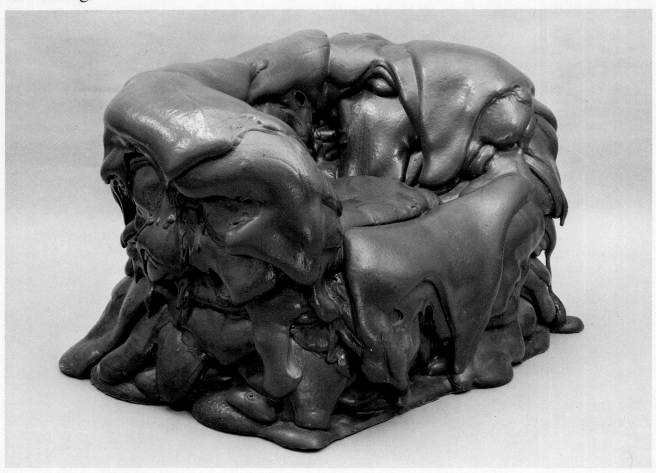

Armchair, Gunnar Aagaard Andersen
1964. Poured urethane foam, 29 1/2 in. x 44 1/4 in. x 35 1/4 in.
Museum of Modern Art, New York.

What Did I Learn?

- **LOOK** back at the artful objects shown in this unit. Which one was your favorite? Why?

- **EXPLAIN** what is unusual about the form of the armchair shown on page 92. Would you like to have the armchair in your house? Why or why not?

- **THINK** about the artworks you created for this unit. In which piece do you think you expressed yourself the most? Is there a piece that only you could have created? Explain.

Dance in Tehauntepec, Diego Rivera
1928. Oil on canvas, 199 x 162 cm.

Designs Old and New

How do artists use tradition to create new works of art?

Diego Rivera, a Mexican artist, showed the culture and the history of Mexico in his artwork. The painting on the left shows a popular Mexican folk dance. In this unit, you will see how artists borrow from the traditions of their own and other cultures. They search for new ways to use ideas from the past.

ABOUT DIEGO RIVERA

Diego Rivera wanted to show his pride in Mexico. Many of his murals are on walls of Mexican public buildings. Some can be seen in buildings in the United States, too.

Traditions in Architecture

How are these buildings alike and different?

These pictures all show famous buildings. The Parthenon, in picture **A**, was a temple. It was built in Greece about 2,500 years ago. Notice the tall marble **columns**.

The Pantheon, in picture **B**, is nearly 2,000 years old. It was built by the Romans. Look at the large, rounded **dome** on top.

A **Parthenon**
Athens, Greece.

B **Pantheon**
Rome, Italy.

Many important buildings in the United States have the same styles as buildings in ancient Greece and Rome. Picture **C** shows the U.S. Capitol, in Washington, D.C. The Supreme Court Building, also in Washington, D.C., is shown in picture **D**.

The art of designing buildings is called **architecture**. Architects often get ideas from the past. Where do you think the architect, Cass Gilbert, got his idea for the Supreme Court Building?

 C U.S. Capitol

D Supreme Court Building

IN THE STUDIO

MATERIALS

- **cardboard**
- **construction paper**
- **tempera paints**
- **paintbrushes**
- **masking tape**
- **scissors**
- **plastic food containers**
- **egg cartons**
- **matboard for base**
- **boxes**

Build a model of a government building for a make-believe country.

1. **Think of a name for a make-believe country. Imagine that you are the architect for its first government building.**

2. **Decide how you can build your model from your materials. Build your model and paint it.**

Artful Arches

Why do you think architects choose certain forms?

Pictures **A** and **B** show structures built by the Romans about 2,000 years ago. The structure in picture **C** was completed in 1965. What shape do these three structures share?

Trace your finger along each **arch** in the pictures. These curved openings were developed by the ancient Romans.

Look at the many arches in picture A. This structure was built to carry water from one place to another. Water flowed along the top. The Arch of Titus, in picture B, was built to honor a great Roman emperor.

The Gateway Arch, in picture C, was built in St. Louis, Missouri. That city is known as the gateway to the western United States. How is the Gateway Arch different from the arches of the ancient Romans?

A Pont du Gard
(Roman aqueduct)
Nîmes, France

B Arch of Titus
Rome, Italy

C Gateway Arch
St. Louis, MO

IN THE STUDIO

MATERIALS

- **cardboard**
- **construction paper or tagboard**
- **tempera paints**
- **paintbrushes**
- **scissors**

Design a gateway for a make-believe country. Use at least one arch in your design.

1. Sketch ideas for a gateway to your country. How many arches will your gateway have?

2. Paint a background scene on cardboard.

3. Make your gateway from construction paper or tagboard. Place it in the scene.

DENVER INTERNATIONAL AIRPORT

Does a building always have to look like a building? What else might it look like?

These pictures show the terminal building of the Denver International Airport in Denver, Colorado. Look at the peaks of the Rocky Mountains in the background.

Denver International Airport, daytime

The architects who designed the building wanted the roof to look like mountains. They think the roof also looks like Native American tepees or curved parts of an airplane. What do you think?

Denver International Airport, nighttime

WHAT DO YOU THINK?

▶ If you didn't know this building was an airport, what would you think it was?

▶ If you designed an airport in your area, what would it look like?

Designing with Symbols

Why do countries create flags, seals, and medals?

A **symbol** is a picture or sign that stands for something. Some symbols stand for important ideas that people share.

The United States flag is a symbol of our country. Each part of the flag has special meaning. The color white stands for purity, red stands for courage, and blue stands for justice. What do the stars and stripes stand for? What has Jasper Johns done with the flag in picture **A**? What do you think this artwork says about our country?

Three Flags, **Jasper Johns**
1958. Encaustic on canvas, 30 7/8 X 45 1/2 in.

Picture **B** shows the flag of Mexico. What objects do you see on the flag? The eagle on the cactus with a snake in its mouth is a symbol that comes from a legend of ancient Mexico.

The eagle is also an American symbol. It is the national bird of the United States. What symbols do you see in picture **C**?

B Mexican flag

C Presidential Medal of Freedom

IN THE STUDIO

MATERIALS

- white paper
- tempera paints
- paintbrushes
- wood dowel
- tape
- ruler
- round plastic lids

Design a flag for your make-believe country. Use a symbol from your country.

1. **Brainstorm ideas about your make-believe country. What symbol or symbols can you use on a flag? How can you arrange the shapes and colors to make a good design?**

2. **Paint your flag. Tape a dowel to one end. Place your flag with your model from Lesson 25.**

Letters and Numbers

How did these artists use letters and numbers in a new way?

Letters are usually used to communicate ideas through written words. In picture **A** Emilio Aguirre [ah•GEE•ray] communicates ideas and feelings through the shapes and colors of letters.

Notice how the shapes that form the letter *Q* come in front of the large *Y*. The *Q* **overlaps** the *Y*. What other overlapping shapes do you see in the picture?

Alpha 1, Emilio Aguirre
1970. Acrylic on canvas.

How do we usually use numbers? In picture **B** Charles Demuth used the figure 5 for its shape. He got his idea from a poem about the number on the side of a fire truck. The poem was by William Carlos Williams. Why do you think the word *Bill* is in the painting?

B

I Saw the Figure 5 in Gold, Charles Demuth
1928. Composition board, 35 1/2 x 30 in.
Alfred Stieglitz Collection,
Metropolitan Museum of Art, New York.

IN THE STUDIO

MATERIALS

- **drawing paper**
- **tempera paints**
- **paintbrushes**
- **black marker**
- **ruler**

Paint a picture that uses a letter or number. Show the letter or number in a new way.

1. **Think about the shape of each letter or number. Sketch some ideas in your sketchbook. How does it look when you turn it sideways or upside down?**

2. **Draw your design on paper. You may want to use a ruler for straight lines. Then paint your design with tempera paints. Choose brush sizes for the effects you want.**

3. **After the paint is dry, use black marker to add details.**

Money Design

The next time you use a coin or dollar bill, stop and take a look at it. You are holding a work of art!

The bills shown here are from different countries of the world. How are they alike? How are they different?

Find the numbers and the letters on each bill. Then look carefully at the pictures. What famous people and objects do you recognize? Which ones would you like to know more about?

One-dollar bills,
United States
of America

1,000 pesos,
Mexico

Twenty-pound note,
Great Britain

בנק ישראל
חמש לירות ישראליות

Five shekels,
Israel

WHAT
DO
YOU
THINK
?

► Why do you think these bills from different countries are alike in so many ways?

► Suppose you were asked to design a brand-new dollar bill for the United States. What would you include in your design and why?

Ways of Life

What can you tell about people's ways of life from looking at these pictures?

People have painted pictures on walls for thousands of years. These **murals** often show people's ways of life.

The mural in picture **A** was painted 1,200 years ago. It was found in a temple of the Maya people in what is today Mexico. The people in white robes at the top are Mayan nobles. They are being entertained by the musicians below. How did the artists make this mural vivid?

 A Section of the Bonampak murals, Maya
Museo Nacional de Antropología, Mexico City.

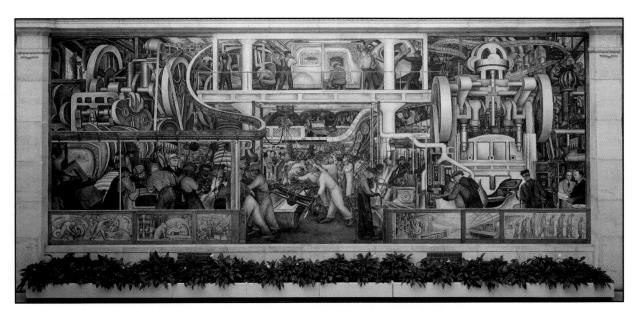

The mural in picture **B** was created by the Mexican artist Diego Rivera. It shows workers in an automobile factory in the 1930s. How is his mural like picture A? How is it different? Diego Rivera studied the ancient art of Mexico. He also went to Italy and studied the murals there. He used what he learned to create his own style. How do you think he felt about modern industry?

 Detroit Industry, **south wall, Diego Rivera**
1932–33. The Detroit Institute of Arts, Detroit.

IN THE STUDIO

MATERIALS

- roll of butcher paper
- drawing paper
- tempera paints
- paintbrushes
- masking tape

Make a class mural showing people at work in a community.

With your group, brainstorm ideas for your part of the mural. Then sketch it. Work with the groups on each side of you to match up your sections. Use tempera paints to paint your mural.

Make It Your Own

What feelings do these artists express about themselves and their heritage?

Yo, **Celia Alvarez Muñoz**
Fujichrome Photograph.
Courtesy of the artist.

In pictures **A** and **B**, the artists used objects to tell about themselves and their culture.

Picture A shows a group of objects that Celia Muñoz [moon•YOHS] arranged and photographed. She called the artwork *Yo,* which means *I* in Spanish. What objects do you see that tell about

110

the artist? What objects tell about her Mexican American heritage?

Picture B shows a group of objects that Betye Saar arranged in a box. The objects in a **persona box** tell about the person who made it. Saar is an African American artist whose work contains both personal and cultural symbols. What can you tell about her?

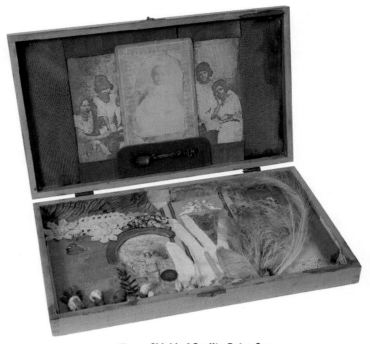

B *Shield of Quality,* **Betye Saar**
1974. Assemblage, 19 X 15 X 2 in., Monique Knowlton Gallery, New York.

IN THE STUDIO

MATERIALS

- box
- fabric
- personal objects
- glue
- scissors

Make your own persona box. Tell about yourself in a pleasing design.

1. **Choose the items for your box. What do you want to show about yourself? How can you share your ideas and feelings about your heritage and personality?**

2. **Arrange the items you have chosen. If you wish, decorate the outside of your box.**

In this unit, you have seen how traditional designs and symbols can be used in many different ways.

Artists often borrow from the traditions of their culture and of other cultures. They can use what they borrow to create something new.

Ojo de Luz (Eye of Light), Oswaldo Viteri
1987. Assemblage on wood,160 X 160 cm. Courtesy of the artist.

What Did I Learn?

- **LOOK** at *Eye of Light* on page 112. The artist used fabric dolls made in villages in his country, Ecuador, to celebrate the culture of his people. How does the artwork do something new and different with traditional objects?

- **DESCRIBE** the simple shapes that form the main design of *Eye of Light*. Find another piece of art in this unit that has a simple, clear design. Tell whether you think the design is strong, and why.

- **LOOK** at the designs that you created or helped create in your artwork for this unit. Which one is your favorite? How did you arrange the parts to make the design pleasing?

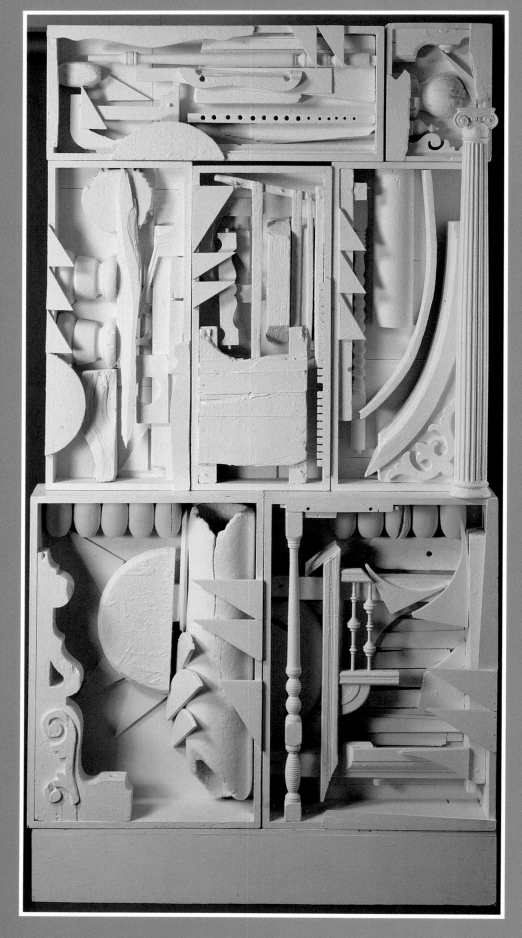

Dawn's Wedding Chapel 1,
Louise Nevelson
1959. Wood painted white, 90 X 51 X 6 in.

Exploring Life's Riches

What kind of art can you enjoy with your senses?

Have you ever seen art that you could almost hear, smell, or taste? Some artists show us new ways to experience art. Louise Nevelson, the creator of this sculpture, used many everyday objects in her artwork. What might the different pieces in her sculpture feel like?

ABOUT LOUISE NEVELSON

Louise Nevelson is best known for her sculptures, which are called assemblages. Each is made of stacked boxes filled with wooden objects. The whole work is painted one color.

New Combinations

How did artists use everyday objects to create these works of art?

Pictures **A**, **B**, and **C** all show three-dimensional art forms called **sculptures**. What do they look like at first glance?

The sculpture in picture A is called *Mocking Bird*. The artist, Margaret Wharton, used parts of wooden chairs to create a sculpture of a bird.

Picture B shows a sculpture called *Bull's Head*. Can you name the objects in this sculpture? The artist, Pablo Picasso, used **found objects**— a bicycle seat and handlebars. He saw something new and different in the shapes of these common objects.

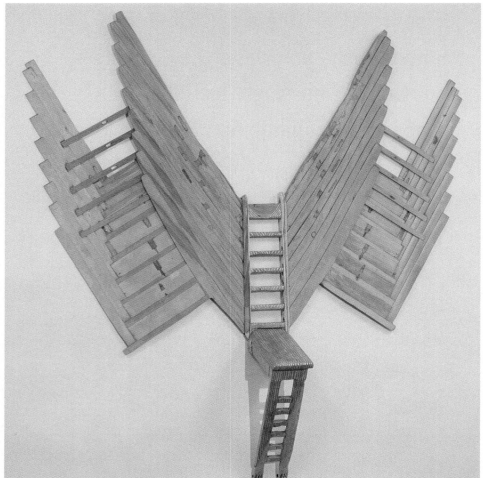

Mocking Bird, **Margaret Wharton**
1981. Partial stained wooden chair, epoxy glue, paint, and wooden dowels, 60 X 60 X 13 in. Collection of the artist.

An eighth-grade student made *Experiment in Orange*, the sculpture in picture C. He made a funny creature out of found objects such as pipes, knobs, handles, and odd pieces of metal.

Imagine how the sculpture looked before it was painted. The artist painted it all one color to give the work **unity**. The parts look as if they belong together.

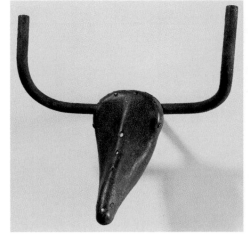

B *Bull's Head,* **Pablo Picasso**
1943. Handlebars and seat of a bicycle.
Musée Picasso, Paris.

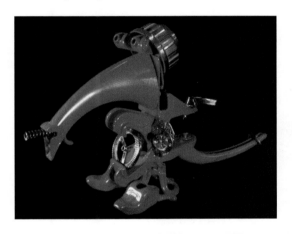

C *Experiment in Orange,*
David Getsy
Found objects.

IN THE STUDIO

MATERIALS

- **found objects**
- **glue**
- **masking tape**

Use found objects to create a sculpture.

Assemble the objects in different ways to create a sculpture with a pleasing form. Glue or tape the objects together to create your sculpture.

A Personal Touch

How do these paintings appeal to the senses?

Pictures **A** and **B** show groups of objects. Each picture has both natural and human-made objects. Each is in an indoor setting. This kind of painting is called a **still life**. Both artists used bright colors to show how the objects look and feel. Can you imagine what the objects in these still lifes might taste like and smell like?

Raspberries and Goldfish, Janet Fish
Oil on canvas, 72 X 64 in.
Metropolitan Museum of Art, New York.

Janet Fish often shows glass objects in her paintings. Notice how the reflections pull your eye from one object to the next in picture A. For picture B, Frank Romero chose objects from his cultural heritage. What makes this combination of objects unusual?

 Still Life with Blue Car, **Frank Romero**
1986. Oil on canvas, 48 X 50 in. Courtesy of the artist.

IN THE STUDIO

MATERIALS

- **natural and human-made objects**
- **oil pastels**
- **drawing paper**

Arrange and draw a still life. Make your drawing appeal to the senses.

1. **Choose natural and human-made objects. Try to use objects that are unusual or have special meaning to you. How do your objects appeal to the senses? Arrange the objects in an interesting way.**

2. **Sketch your still life on the paper. Then use oil pastels to complete your still life. Use bright colors to show what the objects look, feel, smell, and taste like.**

Store Window Displays

Did you ever buy something because you saw it in a store window?

The designers who create window displays are trained to get your attention. They choose just the right items and arrange them in just the right way. Sometimes a window display is designed for a season, a holiday, or another event. Some window displays tell a story. What are the designers of these windows trying to tell you?

WHAT
DO
YOU
THINK
?

▶ **What do you think a window designer thinks about while creating a display?**

▶ **Would the store windows shown here make you want to shop in these stores? Why or why not?**

Finding Textures

How have these artists made common objects look new and different?

Magic Leaves, Susan Kaprov
1997. Oil pastel on rice paper.
Courtesy of the artist.

The artists who created pictures **A** and **B** put paper over objects and rubbed the paper with color. Picture A is a rubbing of natural objects—leaves. Picture B is a rubbing of a human-made object—the metal cover for a coal hole.

Rubbings show an object's texture. Pictures A and B create **visual texture**. This is texture that you see rather than feel. For example, a surface may look rough or smooth, or hard or soft. How would you describe the textures of each of these rubbings?

**Coal hole cover,
Ann Parker and Avon Neal**

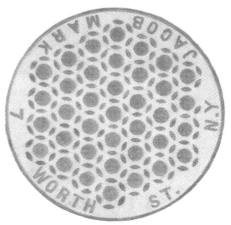

122

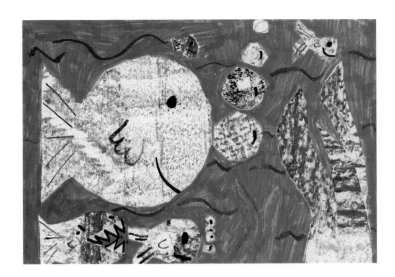

 Student art

IN THE STUDIO

MATERIALS

- drawing paper
- watercolors
- paintbrushes
- scissors
- glue
- tracing paper
- colored pencils or oil pastels

Make a picture that uses rubbings to create visual texture.

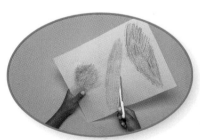

1. **Find some objects with interesting textures. Lay a piece of tracing paper over each object. Rub the paper with a colored pencil or oil pastel.**

2. **Decide which rubbings you want to use in your picture. Cut out the shapes you need from each rubbing.**

3. **Paint a watercolor wash on your drawing paper. When it dries, arrange the cut-out shapes on it to create a picture. Glue the shapes to the paper.**

Textures to Touch

What do you think these works of art would feel like if you touched them?

Pictures **A**, **B**, and **C** have textures that can be felt as well as seen. They are made of fabric, paper, and other materials.

Pictures A and B are collages. A **collage** is a work of art made by gluing pieces of material such as paper and fabric to a flat surface. Each artist used different materials and colors to create **variety**. Variety makes a work of art interesting.

Each collage also shows unity. The pieces are arranged so that they seem to belong together. The repeated colors also help create unity.

The artist who created the work of art in picture C glued fur to a cup, saucer, and spoon. Why do you think she did this? Why do you think artists experiment with new materials?

 No. 237, Anne Ryan
Walker Art Center.

C

Object, **Meret Oppenheim**
1936. Fur-covered cup, saucer, and spoon.
Museum of Modern Art, New York.

B *Porch,* **Tom Wesselmann**
1960. Mixed media and collage, 9 X 10 in.

IN THE STUDIO

MATERIALS

- poster board
- glue
- scraps of fabric, leather, netting, lace
- objects such as yarn, string, rick-rack, buttons
- paper scraps
- scissors

Make a texture collage that is interesting to see and touch.

1. Choose materials for your collage. Do you want to create a design, as in picture A? Or do you want to create a picture, as in picture B?

2. Experiment with arrangements, shapes, and textures. How can you create variety and unity in your work?

3. When you are satisfied with your collage, glue the materials in place.

125

ICE SCULPTURE

Brrrr! Why would someone want to make a sculpture out of ice?

Every winter the city of Plymouth, Michigan, has a celebration called the Ice Sculpture Spectacular. Ice sculptors come from all over the world to carve wonderful and amazing figures. They use tools such as chain saws to shape the blocks of ice.

What do you think of the ice sculptures in these pictures? If you could carve an ice sculpture, what would you make?

◀

Hideki Ota, a professional ice sculptor from Sapporo, Japan

More scenes from Plymouth Ice Sculpture Spectacular

WHAT
DO
YOU
THINK
?

▶ **Which of the ice sculptures do you like best? Why do you like it?**

▶ **What special problems do you think a sculptor might have working with ice?**

127

Musical Inspirations

What feelings about music do these works express?

Picture **A** is a **mural** painted on a wall in a public park. The theme, or idea, of the mural is the spirit of music. John Biggers created the mural to honor a person who was a teacher and choir director. What do you think the choir sounds like? How has John Biggers used lines and shapes to suggest the powerful sound of the music?

 Spirit of Music, John Biggers
About 1984. Acrylic. Christia V. Adair Park, Harris County, TX.

Picture **B** is a collage by Romare Bearden. What instruments do the three musicians play? Look at their faces and hands. What do you think their music sounds like?

B

Three Folk Musicians, **Romare Bearden**
1967. Collage on canvas on board. 50 X 60 in.

IN THE STUDIO

MATERIALS

- **drawing paper**
- **many other kinds of paper, including old magazines, wrapping paper, tissue paper, foil, etc.**
- **scissors**
- **glue**
- **black marker**

Create a cut-paper collage about your favorite musical instrument or kind of music.

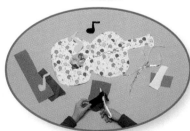

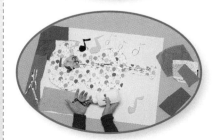

1. **What is your favorite musical instrument or kind of music? On a piece of drawing paper, draw a picture showing your ideas.**

2. **Draw parts of your picture on different kinds of paper. Cut them out.**

3. **Put your pieces on top of the picture you drew. Glue your collage to the paper. Add details with black marker. Can you show how the music sounds?**

Seeing Sounds

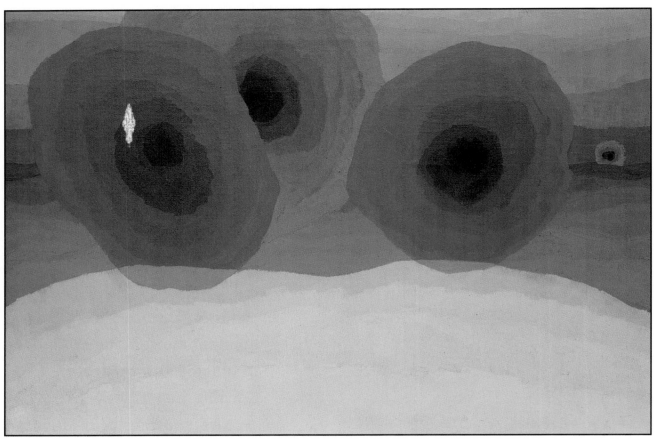

A *Fog Horns,* **Arthur Dove**
1929. 17 3/4 X 25 1/2 in.
Colorado Springs Fine Arts Center, Colorado Springs, CO.

What sounds do you see in these pictures?

The subject of pictures **A** and **B** is sound. The artists used lines, shapes, and colors to create the idea, or impression, of sound. You can't hear the sounds, but can you imagine what they might be?

Picture A is called *Fog Horns*. Have you ever heard the low, dull, sad sound of a boat's fog horn? How did Arthur Dove use shapes and colors to create an impression of that sound?

Blue and Green Music, Georgia O'Keeffe
1919. Oil on canvas, 23 in. X 19 in.
Alfred Stieglitz Collection,
Gift of Georgia O'Keefe, Art Institute of Chicago.

Georgia O'Keeffe named picture B *Blue and Green Music*. What do you suppose she meant? Look at the rhythm created by the lines and shapes in this picture. How do you think blue and green music might sound?

IN THE STUDIO

MATERIALS

- drawing paper
- oil pastels

Use lines, shapes, and color to create an impression of sound.

1. Listen to a sound or some music for a few minutes. What mood does it create? What colors would you use to show that mood? What lines and shapes will create an impression of the sound?

2. Use oil pastels to make your drawing. Press, smudge, and mix the colors to create the impression of the sound you chose.

Artists often try to show how things look, sound, feel, taste, and smell.

In this unit, you have seen some of the new ways artists have invented to appeal to the senses. In doing so, they help us see the beauty and richness of the world around us.

Musical Forms, Georges Braque
1918. Pasted board, corrugated cardboard, charcoal, and gouache on cardboard. 30 3/8 X 37 3/8 in. Philadelphia Museum of Art.

What Did I Learn?

- **LOOK** at the collage on page 132, which is a still life using musical instruments. Georges Braque [BRAHK] made it from different kinds of paper. What senses does the collage appeal to? How is it different from the other still lifes in this unit?

- **EXPLAIN** how the collage titled *Musical Forms* has both unity and variety.

- **LOOK** back at your own artwork for this unit. What new ways of seeing and doing did you learn? Which new art form that you tried did you enjoy most? Why?

- **EXPLAIN** which of your artworks a person could enjoy without the sense of sight.

ART SAFETY

Listen carefully when your teacher tells how to use art materials.

Wear a smock to keep your school clothes clean.

Use the kind of markers and inks **that will not stain your clothes.**

Use tools carefully. Hold sharp objects so that they cannot hurt you or others. Wear safety glasses **if something could get in your eyes.**

Check labels on materials before you use them. Look for the word *nontoxic,* which means "not poisonous."

Cover your skin if you have a cut or scratch. Some art materials, such as clay, can make cuts sting.

Show respect for other students. Walk carefully around their work. Never touch classmates' work without asking first.

Keep your area clean and neat. Clean up spills right away so no one will fall. Put materials back when you finish with them.

Tell your teacher if you have allergies or breathing problems. Some people are allergic to the kinds of dust in some art materials.

Always wash your hands after using art materials.

Trying Ways to Draw

There are lots of ways to draw. You can draw quickly to show the shape of something. You can draw carefully to show just how something looks to you. Try to draw every day. Here are some ideas for drawing.

SCRIBBLE DRAWING

Scribble drawing is a fun way to draw people. It helps you see the **proportions** of a person's body. Proportion is the size of one thing compared to another. For example, the lower part of an arm is about the same length as the upper part.

Find photographs of people playing sports or dancing. Do a scribble drawing of each person. Use a marker. Work very quickly. Spend only a few seconds on each drawing.

• **Scribble the head.** (Don't draw the neck.)
• **Scribble the body.**
• **Scribble the legs and the feet.**
• **Scribble the arms.**

CONTOUR DRAWING

Look closely at something you want to draw. Find the lines that go around shapes. They are called **contours**. Use your finger to trace around the shapes in this picture.

Try making a contour drawing of this picture. Make your drawing bigger than the picture. Look at the picture carefully as you draw. Find all the shapes, edges, and lines.

Now try making contour drawings of some objects. Try drawing a table or a chair. You can even try a contour drawing of a person.

SHADING

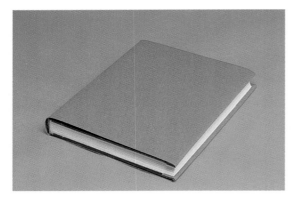

You can show the shape of something in a drawing by using shading. Look at the photograph of a book. Some parts are darker than others. Now look at the drawing of the book. Shading was used to show which parts of the book are darker and which parts are lighter.

The darkness or lightness of a color is its value. Experiment with your pencils. How many values can you make with shading? Try erasing parts of your shading to make bright spots. These are called **highlights**.

Try using shading to draw something simple, like a box. Look closely. Make some areas dark and some areas lighter. Try adding highlights.

CONTOURS AND SHADING

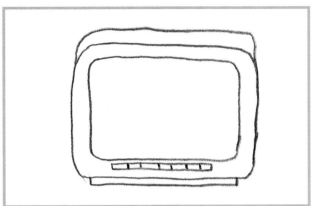

Try adding shading to a contour drawing. Start by doing a contour drawing of something. Pick something with a simple shape, like a television set. Look at it carefully. Find all the lines and shapes. Then look at the object again to see the light and dark areas. Add shading.

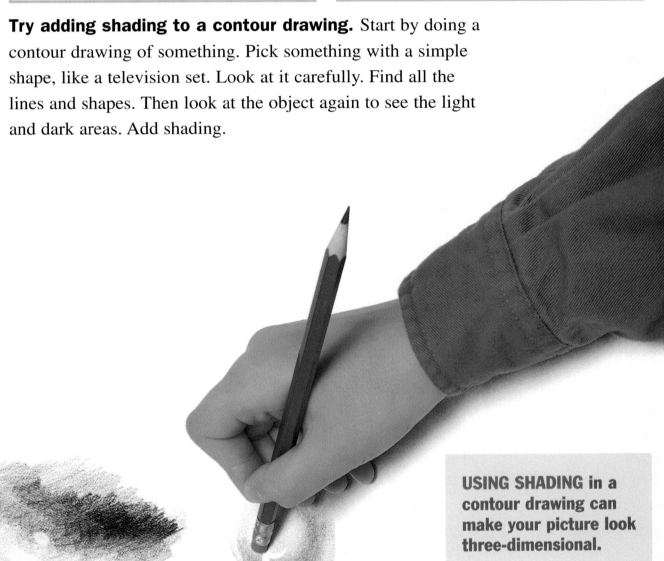

USING SHADING in a contour drawing can make your picture look three-dimensional.

Experimenting with Paint

Trying out ways of painting can help you learn about how artists use color. It can also give you new ideas for using color in your own artwork.

These are some things you should have when you paint: old newspapers to cover your work area, an old shirt to cover your clothes, **tempera paints** or **watercolors**, old dishes or plastic egg cartons for mixing paint, paper, paintbrushes, a jar or bowl of water, and paper towels to wipe your brushes on.

TEMPERA PAINTS

Tempera paints are sometimes called poster paints. They are easy to clean up. The colors are bright and easy to mix.

● GETTING STARTED

Start by dipping your brush into one color. Try different kinds of brushstrokes—long and short, thin and light, wide and heavy.

Now clean your brush and use another color. Twist a brush full of paint on the paper. Roll it, press it, or dab it. On a fresh sheet of paper, make a pattern or a picture using some of these brushstrokes. Try using different colors.

● MIXING COLORS

You can mix tempera paints to make other colors. Put a little of one color in a part of a plastic egg carton. Then add a little of another color.

To make colors darker (**shades**), add black. Add white to make them lighter (**tints**). See how many shades and tints of a single color you can make.

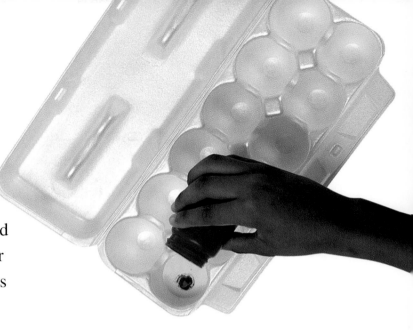

Use what you know about mixing colors to paint your name. Lightly print your name with pencil on a sheet of paper. Leave space between the letters. Paint each letter a different color.

Paint around the letter with a shade or a tint of the same color. If you have room, make more contours around the letters. Use a different shade or tint for each one.

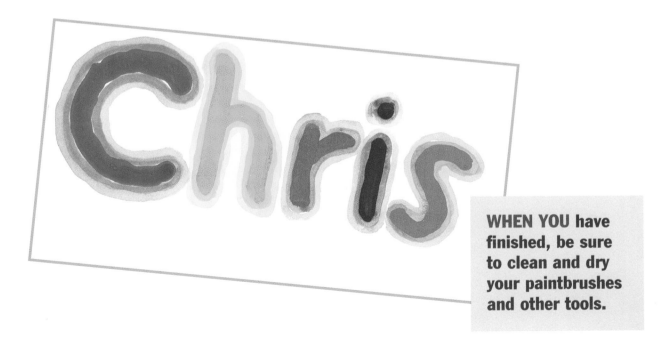

WHEN YOU have finished, be sure to clean and dry your paintbrushes and other tools.

WATERCOLORS

Watercolors usually come in little dry cakes. You add the water! You will need paintbrushes and a jar of clean water to mix with your paint. Paint on thick paper made for watercolors. Keep some paper towels nearby.

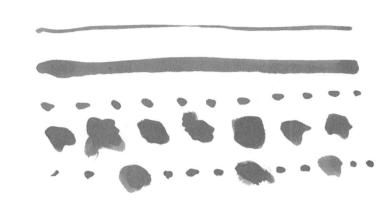

● GETTING STARTED

Put a drop of water on each cake of paint. Then dab your paintbrush in one of the colors. Make thick lines and thin lines. Try dots and blobs. Don't try to make them as dark as the cake of paint. You should be able to see through watercolors.

Rinse your paintbrush in the jar of water and try another color. See what happens to the color when you use a lot of water. Then try using just a little water. Be sure to rinse your brush between colors. If you want part of your painting to be white, don't paint on it. The white comes from the color of the paper.

● MIXING COLORS

Try mixing watercolors right on your paper. Paint with a very wet paintbrush over a brushstroke that is dry. Then try a wet color over another wet color. Put a spot of a wet color so it just touches another wet color. What happens?

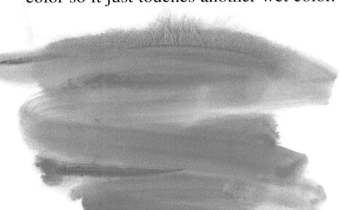

Brush clean water onto the paper. You can use a wide paintbrush or a sponge. Then brush a stroke of color across the wet paper. Let the color spread. This is called a wash.

Now try this. Brush water all over your paper. Make a wash at the top. Use another color to make a wash at the bottom. Now make lots of very wet spots of color on your paper. Use several colors. While the paper is wet, pick up one corner and let the paint run. When the paint is dry, think of a name for your picture.

BE SURE to clean your paintbrushes and your work area when you have finished.

Working with Clay

Clay is a special kind of earth that is used to make many kinds of things. It is easy to shape when it is mixed with water. Clay can be left in the air to dry. It can also be fired, or baked, until hard.

Work with clay on a clean, dry surface.
(A brown paper bag is good.) Store your clay in a plastic bag. Use a little water on your clay if it starts to dry out.

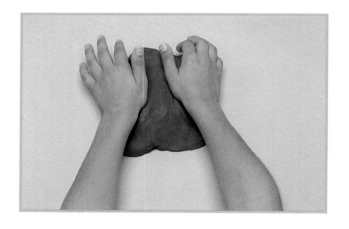

Start working with a piece of clay by getting rid of any air bubbles in it.
Press down hard on it several times, turning it over and pushing the edges in each time. Be sure you don't fold it over, because folding will trap more air inside the clay.

You can use tools to work with clay.
Try using a plastic knife and fork, a stick, a comb, a pencil, burlap, and other things. Tools like these can help you shape your clay and add texture or patterns to it.

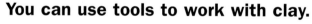

MODELING CLAY

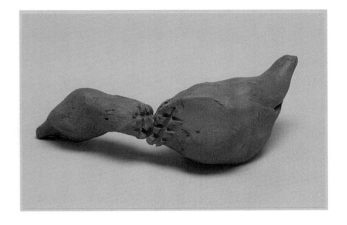

Try making different forms with your clay. Make one of your forms into an animal or a bird. Model, or shape, the form by pinching and pulling the clay.

You can join two pieces together. First, score, or carve lines in, the clay pieces. Then wet them. Press the pieces together. Use water to smooth the seams with your fingers.

Add patterns, textures, or details. Carve designs into the clay with a pencil. Make patterns and textures by pressing objects into the clay and lifting them off. If you change your mind, smooth the clay with your fingers and try something else.

PINCH POTS

To make a pinch pot, form a ball of clay. Press your thumb into the ball to hollow it out. Start pinching the clay from the bottom and work up.

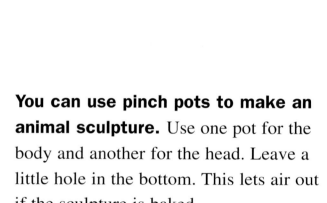

Press and smooth the clay with your fingers. Turn the pinch pot to make the sides even. Use tools to make patterns and textures on the outside.

You can use pinch pots to make an animal sculpture. Use one pot for the body and another for the head. Leave a little hole in the bottom. This lets air out if the sculpture is baked.

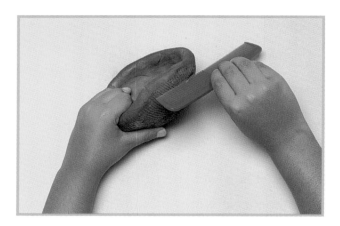

USING COILS

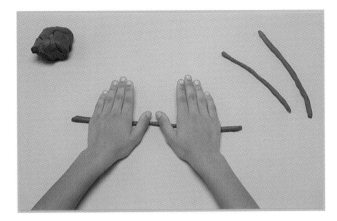

To make a coil pot, roll out many pieces of clay in long rope shapes. Use your whole hand to roll them.

To make the sides of a pot, place a rope of clay around the edge of the bottom. Keep stacking ropes on top of one another. Smooth the inside as you work. You may smooth the outside with water or let the coils show.

To make the bottom of a coil pot, wrap a rope of clay in a circle. Smooth it with your fingers.

You can also use coils to make figures.

WHEN YOU have finished, clean up with damp paper towels.

Exploring Printmaking

When you make a print, you transfer color from one object to another. If you have ever left a fingerprint on a clean glass, you have made a print.

To make prints, you need paint, paper, a paintbrush, newspaper, and paper towels or sponges for cleaning up. Here are some printmaking ideas to try.

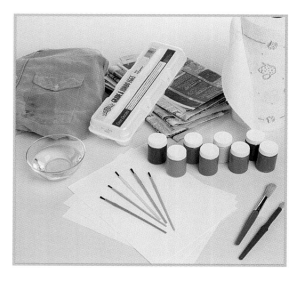

MONOPRINTS

A monoprint is a one-of-a-kind print. Try making a monoprint. Fold a piece of paper in half. Quickly paint a design on one half of the paper. Use thick spots of color. Unfold the paper.

While the paint is wet, fold the blank side of the paper onto the painted side. Rub the paper with your hand. Open it up, and look at your design. It has printed on the other side of the paper!

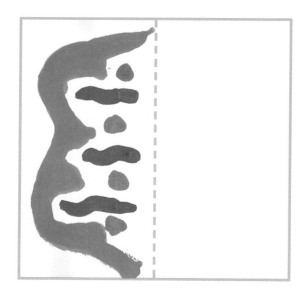

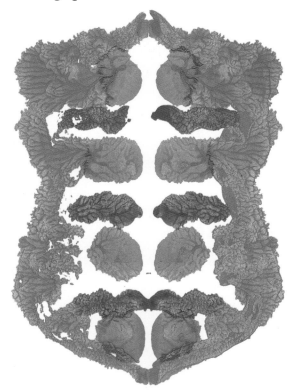

148

STAMP PRINTS

To make stamp prints, you will need an old cookie sheet, paint, and some things to print with. Try using buttons, a straw, a coin, a shell, small boxes, and a paper towel tube.

Put paper towels on the cookie sheet. Spray a little water on them. Then put a little paint on each one. Keep the colors apart. Choose a tool. Press it into the paint. Now press the tool onto a piece of construction paper. Try all your tools.

Use the tools to stamp a pattern. Group the shapes and repeat them. Use different colors. If you want to stamp one shape over another, let one dry first.

BE SURE to clean up when you have finished printing.

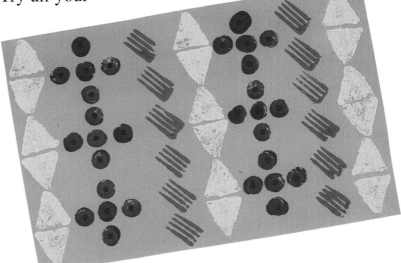

Displaying Your Artwork

Artists like to share their work. They display it in museums or galleries. You can display your artwork too.

DISPLAYING ART PRINTS

Here is a simple way to display pictures. Pick the pictures you like best. Have someone help you put a strong string across a wall. Hang your pictures on the string with paper clips.

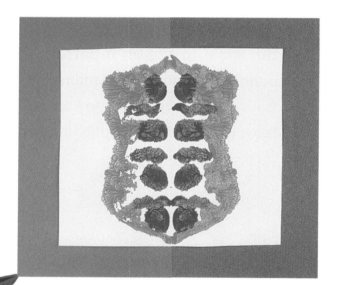

Another way to display a picture is to mount it on colored paper. Choose a color of construction paper that looks good with your art. The paper should be bigger than your picture. You may need to tape two sheets together. Put a spot of glue on the back of each corner of your picture. Glue the picture onto the construction paper.

DISPLAYING SCULPTURES

Find a place to show some of your clay forms or sculptures. Look for a safe place. You may want to use a table in the corner of a room. Now put the artworks you like best on the table.

Move your artworks around. See how they look together. You may want to put your favorite one on a box. Move some other artworks in front of the box. Make sure you can see all the pieces. Ask your friends and family to come look at your work!

ELEMENTS & PRINCIPLES

Have you ever thought of art as a language?

Art communicates feelings, stories, and ideas. The **elements of art and principles of design** are like the words and sentences of the language of art. They are the tools artists use to communicate.

This section will show you the elements and principles. You may want to return to this section now and then to help you think about art.

As you learn more about the elements and principles, try to notice line, shape, and pattern all around you. Think about how artists, including yourself, use color, balance, and texture. Learn to look for and use the language of art.

Line

horizontal

straight

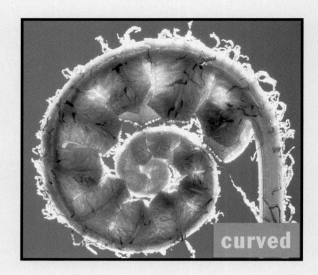

curved

diagonal

zigzag

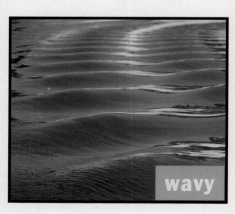

wavy

vertical

Texture

soft

rough

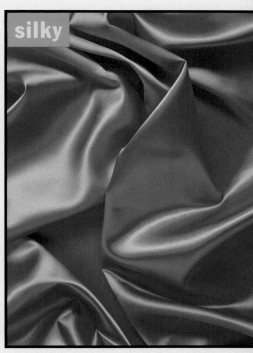

silky

smooth

bumpy

Shape

geometric

circle

oval

triangle

rectangle

square

symbols and letters

organic

Form

geometric

sphere

pyramid

cone

cube

organic

cylinder

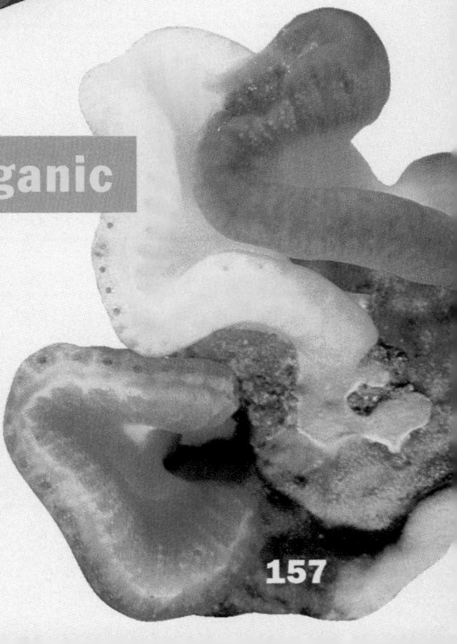

Color

complementary

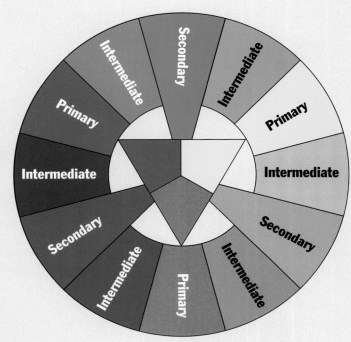

warm

cool

Value

shadows

light to dark

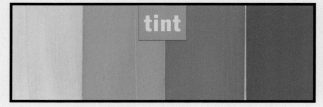

tint

shade

positive, negative

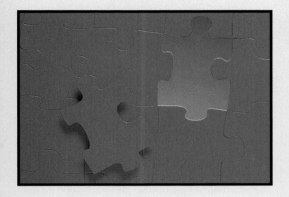

background

middle ground

foreground

proportion

point of view

eye level

worm's eye

bird's eye

Unity

repeated lines,
textures, colors,
shapes, forms

Variety

different lines, textures,
colors, shapes, forms

Emphasis

Pattern

Movement and Rhythm

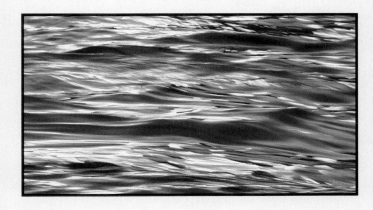

Balance

asymmetrical

symmetrical

physical balance

GALLERY OF ARTISTS

Emilio Aguirre (1929–) United States, painter. Emilio Aguirre [ah•GEE•ray] was born and grew up in Texas. He served in the Korean War and wrote a book about his experiences. Aguirre's paintings show a variety of subjects and styles, from traditional to modern.
page 104

Romare Bearden (1912–1988) United States, collagist. Romare Bearden is best known for his collages. They tell stories of his own experiences and those of other African Americans. Bearden often used his childhood memories and his love of jazz and folk music in his art.
pages 25, 129

Harrison Begay (1917–) United States, painter. Harrison Begay was born in Arizona and studied art at the Santa Fe Indian School. After serving in World War II, Begay returned to the Navajo reservation to work as a painter.
page 77

Thomas Hart Benton (1889–1975) United States, painter. Thomas Hart Benton began his career as a newspaper cartoonist. He later became known for his paintings of rural America as well as Biblical and historical subjects. Benton's murals can be found in many museums and public buildings in the United States. **page 62**

Albert Bierstadt (1830–1902) United States, painter. Born in Germany, Albert Bierstadt [BEER•stat] spent his childhood in Massachusetts. After studying art in Germany and Italy as a young man, he returned to the United States. He is best known for his large landscapes of the American West.
page 38

John Biggers (1924–) United States, painter. John Biggers is a former teacher who believes that art can help African Americans better understand their culture. His paintings, drawings, and murals have been widely shown and have won many awards. **page 128**

Eugene Boudin
(1824–1898) France, painter. Eugene Boudin [boo•DAN] was one of the first landscape painters to paint in the open air. He is best known for his beach and nature scenes. **page 42**

Georges Braque
(1882–1963) France, painter. Georges Braque [BRAHK] is considered one of the founders of the Cubist movement. His paintings show geometric shapes and colors that give his work a peaceful feeling. He is well known for his still lifes. **page 132**

Charles Burchfield
(1893–1967) United States, painter. Charles Burchfield grew up in Ohio. In the 1920s and 1930s, he painted the farms, villages, and cities of the Midwest. His later work celebrated the world of nature. **page 19**

Alexander Calder
(1898–1976) United States, painter/sculptor. Alexander Calder is best known for his mobiles. Calder's work also includes fabric designs, jewelry, prints, and paintings. **page 85**

Emily Carr
(1871–1945) Canada, painter. Emily Carr traveled to western Canada to paint the landscapes and people of the Indian villages on the coast. Carr was sixty-five when she had her first solo art exhibit. **page 39**

Mary Cassatt
(1844–1926) United States and France, painter/printmaker. Mary Cassatt [kuh•SAT] was born in Pennsylvania but spent most of her adult life in France. Her printmaking was strongly influenced by Japanese prints. Her paintings were most often of human subjects. She especially liked to paint women and children. **page 58**

Marc Chagall
(1887–1985) Russia and France, painter/ illustrator/stained-glass artist. Marc Chagall

[shuh•GAHL] painted in the Cubist style. He ignored the law of gravity to express his sense of fantasy. **pages 14, 30**

 **Louisa Chase** (1951–) United States, painter. Louisa Chase's favorite subjects include waves, trees, storm clouds, waterfalls, and mountains. Her brightly colored landscape paintings show the power of nature. **page 49**

 **Christo and Jeanne-Claude** (1935–) United States, environmental artists. Christo and Jeanne-Claude began making art in the 1950s and "packaging" buildings and wrapping coastlines in the 1960s. They later created many more large-scale temporary works of art in both rural and urban settings. **page 40**

 **Charles Demuth** (1883–1935) United States, painter. Charles Demuth is best known as a leader of the Precisionist Movement. This group of painters showed industrial scenes in an attractive and decorative way. **page 105**

 **William Doriani** (1891–?) Russia and the United States, painter. William Doriani was born in Russia but spent his childhood in the United States. As a young man, he studied music. He was a successful opera singer in Europe. During this time he became interested in painting. When he moved back to the United States, he began a career in painting. **page 64**

 **Arthur Dove** (1880–1946) United States, painter / collagist. Arthur Dove first studied commercial art. His interest in how objects *feel* led him to work in collage as well as painting. **page 130**

 **Janet Fish** (1938–) United States, painter. Janet Fish grew up wanting to be an artist like her mother and grandfather. Her realistic paintings show light reflected through glass, water, and mirrors. Because changes in weather affect the way colors look, Fish always works on two paintings at the same time—one for cloudy days and one for sunny days. **page 118**

Pedro Friedeberg

(1937–) Italy and Mexico, sculptor/ muralist. Pedro Friedeberg [FREED•berg] designed his "foot-hand" chairs to echo the massive forms of Mexican pyramids. His works can be seen in museums and public buildings in several countries. **page 84**

Paul Gauguin

(1848–1903) France, painter. Paul Gauguin [goh•GAN] grew up in France. He was a sailor in the French navy and a stockbroker before deciding to become a painter at the age of thirty-five. In 1895 Gauguin moved to the tropical island of Tahiti. He lived and painted in the tropics for the rest of his life. **page 32**

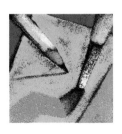

Miki Hayakawa

United States, painter. Miki Hayakawa [MEE•kee hy•uh•KOW•uh] was born in Japan but studied art in California. Her works have been shown at state and county fairs in California, where they have won several prizes. **page 31**

Palmer Hayden

(1893–1973) United States, painter. Palmer Hayden was born in Virginia and studied art in France. When he returned to the United States, he joined the African American community in the Harlem neighborhood of New York City. He painted pictures of African American life, experiences, and folklore. **page 59**

David Hockney

(1937–) United States, mixed media. Born in England, artist David Hockney now lives in southern California. He was eleven years old when he decided he wanted to be an artist. Hockney has said, "The smallest event can become a story if you tell it in the right way." **page 56**

Winslow Homer

(1836–1910) United States, painter/illustrator. Winslow Homer was fascinated by the ocean. He painted many works that show the coasts of Maine (where he lived), the Bahamas, Cuba, and Florida. Many of his works show humans struggling against powerful seas. **page 48**

Edward Hopper (1882–1967) United States, painter. Edward Hopper is known for his realistic scenes of city streets, country roads, and buildings. His paintings usually have a sad and lonely mood. **page 18**

Inga Hunter (1938–) Australia, fabric artist. Inga Hunter creates many types of fabric art, but she is best known for her batiks. She was the founder and president of the Australian Batik Association. **page 74**

Gwen John (1876–1939) France, painter. Born in Wales, Gwen John spent most of her life in Paris. She produced more than 1,000 drawings and watercolors and about 200 oil paintings. **page 22**

Jasper Johns (1930–) United States, painter/printmaker/sculptor. The works of Jasper Johns include a wide variety of paintings, prints, and sculpture. Johns has created realistic sculptures of objects such as a flashlight or a can of paintbrushes. In the 1960s and 1970s, he began incorporating real objects into large and complex paintings. **page 102**

Ogata Kenzan (1663–1743) Japan, painter/calligrapher/potter. Ogata Kenzan [oh•GAHT•ah KEN•zahn] was a quiet man. His work was said to have a "freedom of design" and a "poetry of mood." **page 44**

Paul Klee (1879–1940) Switzerland, painter. The colorful works of the Swiss artist Paul Klee [KLAY] have sometimes been described as childlike. He created many paintings, drawings, and etchings. His parents were both musicians. Klee himself was a professional violinist before becoming an artist. **pages 17, 71**

Jacob Lawrence (1917–) United States, painter. Jacob Lawrence grew up in the Harlem neighborhood of New York City. Many of his paintings show the history of African Americans. He uses simple, bold forms to make his subjects seem like the heroes of legends. **page 54**

Sharon Maczko United States, painter. California artist Sharon Maczko chooses objects and sets up scenes, which she then paints in watercolor. While creating these imaginary worlds, she explores her feelings and memories. She has said that she likes to show "something happening or the feeling that an event is about to happen" in her art. **page 72**

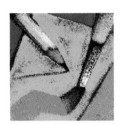

George Washington Maher (1864–1926) United States, architect. George Washington Maher was part of an important group of architects known as the "prairie school." They worked in Chicago. **page 78**

John Marin (1870–1953) United States, painter/etcher. John Marin [MAHR•in] was trained as an architect. He used watercolors to paint landscapes and seascapes of the coast of Maine. **page 42**

Henri Matisse (1869–1954) France, painter. Henri Matisse [ahn•REE ma•TEES] was a lawyer whose hobby was painting. He soon became one of the most important artists of the twentieth century. Matisse was the leader of a group of artists who used bright colors and strong brushstrokes. This was considered so shocking that the artists were known as the Fauves [FOHVS], or "wild beasts." **page 16**

Melissa Miller (1951–) United States, painter. Melissa Miller was born in Texas and studied art in New Mexico. She is known for the energy of her paintings, her pictures of animals, and the way her art tells stories. **page 51**

Celia Alvarez Muñoz (1937–) United States, photographer. Celia Muñoz [moon•YOHS]. was born and grew up in El Paso, Texas. She studied printmaking, advertising, and photography. Muñoz sets up objects to create an environment, which she photographs. Her art often tells a story and reflects the meeting of different cultures. **page 110**

Louise Nevelson (1900–1988) United States, sculptor. Born in Russia, Louise Nevelson moved to Maine as a young girl. She studied music and dance but was most interested in art. Louise Nevelson is well known for her large, assembled sculptures. Some of them take up whole walls and entire rooms. **page 114**

Georgia O'Keeffe
(1887–1986) United States, painter. Georgia O'Keeffe grew up on a farm in Wisconsin. She knew she wanted to be an artist by the age of thirteen. O'Keeffe later became one of the most important American artists of the early twentieth century. Many of her most famous paintings show close-up views of flowers. Art critics have praised the bold shapes and intense colors of her paintings. **page 131**

Mattie Lou O'Kelley
(1908–1997) United States, painter. Mattie Lou O'Kelley began painting at the age of sixty. Her works show memories of her childhood experiences. In a book about her early life, she wrote, "I like to sit on the porch with my pencil and tablet, sketching chickens, roosters, horses, and other farm things, and painting portraits of people I've made up." **page 28**

Meret Oppenheim
(1913–1985) Switzerland, sculptor/ painter. Best known for her fur-covered cup, saucer, and spoon, Meret Oppenheim [AHP•en•hym] is known as a Surrealist artist. She also produced unusual paintings and woodcuts. **page 125**

Ann Parker
United States, photographer. Ann Parker wanted to examine and preserve the history of early American stone and metal carving. Her work includes rubbings of surfaces in New York City, such as coal holes and manhole covers. **page 122**

Pablo Picasso
(1881–1973) Spain, painter. Pablo Picasso was one of the greatest artists of the twentieth century. His works changed the way people thought about art. He helped found a movement in painting called *Cubism*. Cubist painters use basic geometric shapes instead of natural ones. Pablo Picasso was influenced by the style of African sculpture. **page 117**

Patricia Polacco (1944–) United States, author/illustrator. Many of Patricia Polacco's [puh•LAHK•oh] earliest memories are about storytelling in her family. Besides her writing and illustrating, Patricia Polacco is also an expert in Greek and Russian icons and works with museums to help restore them. **page 60**

Diego Rivera (1886–1957) Mexico, muralist. Diego Rivera is famous for his murals. Most are in Mexico City, but quite a few can be seen in the United States, along with many of his smaller paintings and drawings. Rivera was only ten years old when he began taking art courses in Mexico City. He once said, "In my work, I tell the story of my nation, Mexico—its history, its Revolution, its amazing Indian past, and its present-day popular traditions." **pages 94, 109**

Frank Romero (1941–) United States, painter. Frank Romero has lived and worked in Mexico, New Mexico, and California. He says, "My work is about the things I like and the things I enjoy doing. It is about color, the application of paint, the way things feel." **page 119**

Anne Ryan (1889–1954) United States, writer/painter. Anne Ryan had already written a novel and a book of poems before becoming a painter. Later in her life, she began making collages. **page 124**

Betye Saar (1926–) United States, sculptor/collagist. Growing up in California, Betye Saar collected "treasures" such as beads, stones, and bits of glass. As an adult artist, Saar still collects common treasures that she finds near and far. She uses these found objects to create new works of art. **page 111**

John Schoenherr (1935–) United States, illustrator/painter. John Schoenherr has illustrated more than forty children's books and hundreds of science fiction book covers. He is also known for his many wildlife paintings. **page 46**

Charles Searles
(1937–) United States, painter. Charles Searles's works celebrate his African American heritage. Born in Philadelphia, he traveled to West Africa and created a series of paintings that express the rhythms, movements, and meanings in African dance. **page 65**

Truong Thi Thinh
(1928–) Vietnam, painter. Truong Thi Thinh [CHUNGK TEE TIN] came to the United States in 1986. She uses strong colors in her paintings to show the mystery and magic of her homeland. **page 24**

Mark Tobey
(1890–1976) United States, painter. As a young man, Mark Tobey learned the art of Chinese brushwork called calligraphy. He developed a style called "whitewriting," in which he drew white lines similar to the lines in calligraphy. The Broadway area of New York City, with its bright lights and energy, is the subject of many of his paintings. **page 36**

Chris Van Allsburg
(1949–) United States, author/illustrator. Chris Van Allsburg is well known for the fantasy in his writing and illustrations. He has won two Caldecott medals for his books. **pages 12, 20**

Vincent van Gogh
(1853–1890) Holland, painter. Vincent van Gogh [van GOH] sold only one painting when he was alive. But today he is recognized as one of the most famous painters in the world. He used bright colors and thick oil paint. His brushstrokes are easy to see. Van Gogh's paintings show his strong feelings about the beauty of nature. **page 22**

Oswaldo Viteri (1931–) Ecuador, painter/ multimedia artist. Oswaldo Viteri studied architecture, art, and folklore. His work reflects the Hispanic-American cultural heritage of Latin America. Viteri's artworks have been shown all over the world. **page 112**

Tom Wesselmann (1931–) United States, collagist. One day Tom Wesselmann found a painted board in a gutter. He put it together with other found objects to create a collage of a figure seated by a window. This was one of his first works. **page 125**

Margaret Wharton (1943–) United States, sculptor. Margaret Wharton was born in Virginia. Her sculpture, which includes chair sculpture, has been shown all over the United States. **page 116**

Betty Woodman (1930–) United States, ceramic artist. Betty Woodman studied art in New York and in Italy. Her work can be found in many museums. **page 83**

Wyland (1956–) United States, painter. Wyland has dived all over the world to study ocean life for his paintings. He has painted thirty-three life-size Whaling Walls. **page 50**

Wang Yani (1975–) China, painter. Born in China to a family of artists, Wang Yani began painting at the age of two. At three, she amazed her family with her incredible paintings of cats and monkeys. At four, she had her first major art show. And by the age of six, she had created 4,000 paintings. Her works have been shown throughout the world. **page 34**

Melanie Yazzie United States, printmaker/ sculptor. Melanie Yazzie [YAW•zee] grew up on a Navajo reservation in Arizona. She has traveled widely and worked on art projects with people in many parts of the world. She says that she prefers art that is gentle on the earth. Besides printmaking, she likes ceramics because natural clay is found all over the world, and most cultures have used it to create art. **page 45**

GLOSSARY

The Glossary contains important art terms and their definitions. Each word is respelled as it would be in a dictionary. When you see this mark ´ after a syllable, pronounce that syllable with more force than the other syllables.

add, **ā**ce, c**ä**re, p**ä**lm; **e**nd, **ē**qual; **i**t, **ī**ce; **o**dd, **ō**pen, **ô**rder; t**o͝o**k p**o͞o**l; **u**p, b**û**rn; y**o͞o** as *u* in *fuse*; **oi**l; p**ou**t; ə as *a* in *above*, *e* in *sicken*, *i* in *possible*, *o* in *melon*, *u* in *circus*; **ch**eck; ri**ng**; **th**in; **th**is; **zh** as in *vision*

arch [ärch] Curved opening often used in architecture.

arch

architecture [är´kə•tek•chər] The art of designing buildings.

architecture

asymmetrical balance [ā•sə•me´tri•kəl ba´ləns] The look of a design in which things are not placed the same way in relation to a center line.

background [bak´ground] The part of an artwork that appears farthest away from the viewer.

balance [ba´ləns] The arrangement of elements in a work of art. Two kinds of balance are *symmetrical balance* and *asymmetrical balance* (*See also* asymmetrical balance, symmetrical balance.)

batik [bə•tēk´] A method of hand-printing designs on cloth by putting wax on the parts not to be dyed.

batik

center of interest [sen´tər əv in´trest] The part of an artwork that stands out.

cityscape [si´tē•skāp] A painting or drawing showing a view of a city.

collage [kə•lazh´] A work of art created by gluing bits of paper, fabric, scraps, photographs, or other materials to a flat surface.

color [kəl´ər] The aspect of objects caused by the way they reflect or absorb light. Color is an element of design.

column [kä´ləm] A tall post used in or around buildings for support.

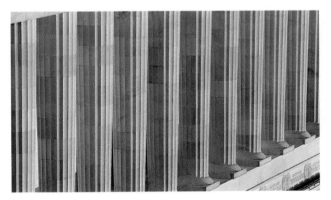

column

contrast [kän´trast] The difference between the colors or other qualities of two things that makes one or both stand out.

cool colors [kōōl kəl´ərz] The family of colors that goes from greens through blues to violets. (*See also* warm colors.)

design [di•zīn´] A plan or sketch to be used as a pattern for making something.

detail [di•tāl´] A part of an object or scene that can be seen most clearly close-up.

diagonal line [dī•a´gə•nəl līn] A line that slants.

dome [dōm] A rounded shape on a roof or forming a roof.

dome

emphasis [em´fə•sis] Giving importance to a certain part of an artwork by using different shapes, lines, and colors.

fantasy [fan´tə•sē] A story or idea that is imagined or could not be true.

fibers [fī´bərz] Threads or yarns that make up a fabric.

foreground [fôr´ground] The part of an artwork that looks closest to the viewer.

form [fôrm] The three-dimensional shape of an object.

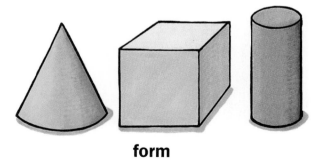

form

found objects [found ob´jikts]
Common objects used in new ways.

found objects

horizontal [hor•ə•zänt´əl] Straight from
side to side; parallel to the horizon.

industrial designer [in•dus´trē•əl
di•zī´nər] Artist who creates useful
items in interesting forms, usually to be
mass-produced.

intermediate colors [in•tər•mē´dē•ət
kəl´ərz] Colors that are created by
mixing a primary color with a secondary
color. (*See also* primary colors,
secondary colors.)

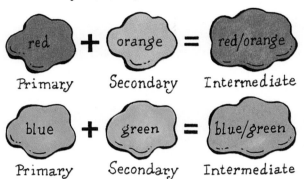

intermediate colors

landscape [land´skāp] An outdoor
scene that shows the beauty of nature.

line [līn] The connection between two
or more points.

loom [lo͞om] A frame that holds a weaving.

loom

midline [mid´līn] An imaginary line down the middle of a painting or drawing.

mola [mō´lə] A colorful design made of layers of cloth.

mola

mood [mo͞od] An overall feeling or emotion.

mosaic [mō•zā´ik] A picture or design formed with small pieces of colored paper, glass, tile, stone, or similar materials.

mosaic

mural [myo͝or´əl] A very large painting that covers a wall. It can be painted right on the wall or on paper, canvas, or wood to be attached to the wall.

mural

overlapping [ō´vər•lap•ing] A way to make one shape or part of an artwork cover up some part or all of another.

overlapping

papier-mâché [pā•pər•mə•shā´] An art material made of paper torn into strips or made into pulp and mixed with art paste.

pattern [pa´tərn] Repeating lines, shapes, or colors in a design.

persona box [pər•sō´nə boks] A box containing objects that tell about the artist who made it.

photograph [fō´tə•graf] A picture taken with a camera.

pinch pot [pinch pät] A clay container formed by pinching, pulling, and pressing the clay.

pinch pot

portrait [pôr´trət] A picture of a person, several people, or an animal.

primary colors [prī´mer•ē kəl´ərz] The colors red, yellow, and blue. They can be mixed together to form other colors. (*See also* intermediate colors, secondary colors.)

print [print] A mark or picture made when a flat surace such as paper is pressed against an object or printing block covered with wet color.

print

proportion [prə•pôr´shən] The size of one thing compared to the size of another thing.

rhythm [ri´thəm] The regular repetition of lines, shapes, colors, or patterns in a work of art.

rhythm

sculpture [skəlp´chər] A three-dimensional piece of art made by carving, modeling, or assembling.

seascape [sē´skāp] A view or picture of the ocean or sea.

secondary colors [se´kən•der•ē kəl´ərz] The colors orange, green, and violet. These are created by combining two of the three primary colors. (*See also* intermediate colors, primary colors.)

self-portrait [self•pôr´trət] A painting of the artist made by the artist.

shade [shād] A color to which black has been added to make the base color darker. (*See also* tint.)

shading [shād´ing] The lines, dots, or dark colors that show shadows, depth, or darkness in a picture or drawing.

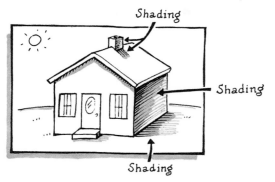

shading

shape [shāp] A two-dimensional figure outlined by lines or a change in color or shading.

space [spās] The distance, area, or depth shown in a work of art. Also, the open parts between or inside shapes. Space is an element of design.

still life [stil līf] An arrangement of mostly nonliving objects shown in an artwork.

symbol [sim´bəl] A picture or sign that stands for something else.

symmetrical balance [sə•me´tri•kəl ba´ləns] The look of a design in which things are placed the same way in relation to a center line.

tempera paints [tem´pə•rə pānts] Bright-colored paints that are easy to mix. They are also called *poster paints*.

texture [teks´chər] The way a surface looks and feels, such as rough or smooth.

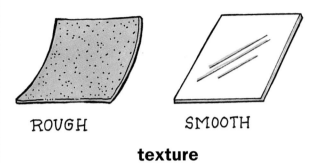

ROUGH   SMOOTH

texture

three-dimensional [thrē•də•men´shə•nəl] Having height, width, and depth. A sculpture is three-dimensional, but a drawing is two-dimensional because it does not have depth. (*See also* two-dimensional.)

tint [tint] A color to which white has been added to make the base color lighter. (*See also* shade.)

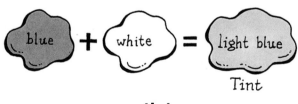

blue + white = light blue

Tint

tint

two-dimensional [tōo•də•men´shə•nəl] Having length and width but not depth; flat. (*See also* three-dimensional.)

unity [yōō´nə•tē] The balance and organization of the parts of an artwork that makes them look as if they belong together.

value [val´yōō] The lightness or darkness of a color.

value

variety [və•rī´ə•tē] An assortment of lines, colors, forms, shapes, or textures in a work of art.

vertical [vər´ti•kəl] Straight up and down.

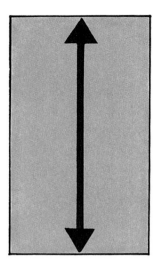

vertical

visual rhythm [vi´zhə•wəl ri´thəm] A rhythm created by the repetition of shapes, colors, and patterns.

visual rhythm

visual texture [vi´zhə•wəl teks´chər] A texture that can be seen rather than felt.

warm colors [wärm kəl´ərz] The family of colors that goes from reds through oranges to yellows. (*See also* cool colors.)

warp [wôrp] In a weaving, the fibers that run from the top to the bottom. (*See also* weft.)

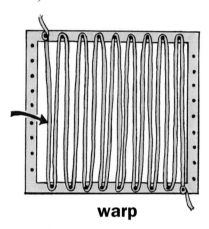

warp

watercolor [wô´tər•kəl•ər] A kind of paint made by mixing powdered colors with a binding agent and water. The term also refers to a painting done with watercolors.

weaving [wēv´ing] Artwork created by lacing together or interlocking fibers, such as strands of thread, yarn, or other materials, on a loom.

weft [weft] In a weaving, the fibers that run from side to side. (*See also* warp.)

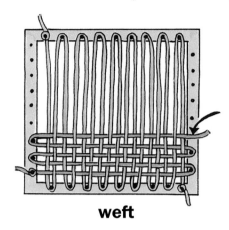

weft

ARTISTS & ARTWORKS

INDEX

ACKNOWLEDGMENTS

PHOTO CREDITS
Page Placement Key: (t)-top (c)-center (b)-bottom (l)-left (r)-right

Cover: Superstock

Table of Contents:
4 Reading Time, Mattie Lou O'Kelley, Decatur Georgia, 1981, oil on canvas, Photography courtesy of the Museum of Modern Folk Art, New York; From the book "Mattie Lou O'Kelley: Folk Artist", © 1989 by Mattie Lou O'Kelley. Used with permission of Little Brown ans Company.; 5 (l) Denver Art Museum, Purchased with the funds from the National Endowment for the Arts Matching Fund ans Alliance for Contemporary Art.; 5(r) George R.Nutter Fund, courtesy, Museum of Fine Arts, Boston.; 6 Courtesy of Sharon Maczko; 7 (l) Gift of Miss Ima Hogg. The Museum of Fine Arts, Houston.; 7 (r) From the book MOLAS, Folk Art of the Cuna Indians, by Ann Parker and Avon Neal; 8 Superstock;

Front Matter:

Harcourt Brace & Company:
13 (l) (bl) (b) Sheri O'Neal; 13 (t) (tr) (c)Weronica Ankarorn;

Other: 11 Richard Nowitz; 12 (t) (b) Courtesy of Houghton Mifflin Company;

Unit 01
Harcourt Brace & Company:
19, 29, & 31 (b) Weronica Ankarorn; 21 (b) Harcourt Brace & Company Photo Library;

Other:
14 Art Resource/Stedelijk Museum, Amsterdam, ©1997 Artists Rights Society (ARS), N.Y./ADAGP, Paris; 15 UPI/Corbis-Bettmann; 16 Photograph © 1996. The Detroit Institute of Arts, City of Detroit Purchase. © 1997 Succession H. Matisse, Paris/Artists Rights Society (ARS), N.Y.; 17 Kunstmuseum Bern, Paul-Klee-Stiftung, Bern; 18 Museum of Modern Art,New York City/Superstock; 19 (t) Archer M. Huntington Art Gallery, The University of Texas at Austin, Gift of Mari and James A. Michener,1991. Photo by George Holmes; 20, 21(b) Houghton Mifflin Company; 22 (t) Van Gogh Museum, Amsterdam, Netherlands/Superstock; 22 (b) SAG52909, A Corner of the Artist's Room, Paris by Gwen John (1876-1939) Sheffield City Art Galleries/Bridgeman Art Library, London, © 1998 Artist Rights Society (ARS), New York/DACS, London; 24 Courtesy of Smithsonian Institution Traveling Exhibition Service & Truong Thi Thinh; 25 Carnegie Museum of Art, Pittsburg. Gift of Mr. and Mrs. Ronald R. Davenport and Mr. and Mrs. Milton A. Washington, 84.63, (c)1998 Romare Bearden Foundation/Licensed by VAGA, New York, NY; 26 Jose L. Pelaez/The Stock Market; 26-27 Magnum Photos; 27 Norman McGrath/Esto Photographics; 28 Reading Time, Mattie Lou O'Kelley, Decatur Georgia, 1981, oil on canvas, Photography courtesy of the Museum of American Folk Art, New York; From the book "Mattie Lou O'Kelley: Folk Artist", © 1989 by Mattie Lou O'Kelley. Used with permission of Little Brown and Company.; 30 Marc Chagall, Paris Through the Window, 1913, The Solomon R. Guggenheim Foundation, New York. Photograph by David Heald © The Solomon R. Guggenheim Foundation, New York FN37.438, ©1997 Artists Rights Society (ARS), N.Y./ADAGP, Paris; 31 (t) Reprinted by permission of Bram and Sandra Dijkstra; 32 Planet Art;

Unit 02:
Harcourt Brace & Company:
37 (b), 43, 45 (b), 49 (b), 51 (b), & 53 Weronica Ankarorn;

Other: 34 The Nelson-Atkins Museum of Art; 35 From A Young Painter:The Life and Paintings of Wang Yani by Zheng Zhensun and Alice Low. ©1991 Byron Preiss Visual Publications, Inc. and New China Pictures Company. Photographs by Zheng Zhensun © 1991 New China Picyures Company.; 36 The Metropolitan Museum of Art, Arthur Hoppock Hearn Fund, 1942. © 1996 Artists Rights Society (ARS), N.Y./Pro Litteris, Zurich; 37 (t) John Button Yellow Sunset 1963, watercolor on paper, 8 x 12" courtesy Fischbach Gallery, New York. Photo credit: Plakke/Jacobs, New York; 38 The Metropolitan Museum of Art, Rogers Fund, 1907. (07.123); 39 Emily Carr, Mountain Forest, VAG 42.3.27, Photo:Courtesy Vancouver Art Gallery, Trevor Mills, VAG.; 40 (t) Copyright: Christo, Photo: Sylvia Volz; 40 (b) © Christo, 1972, Photo by Harry Shunk; 41 © Christo, 1972, Photo by Harry Shunk; 42 (t) Superstock; 42 (b) Archer M. Huntington Art Gallery, The University Of Texas at Austin, Gift of Mari and James A. Michener. Photo by George Holmes; 44 William Sturgis Bigelow Collection, Courtesy, Museum of Fine Arts, Boston; 45 (tl) Glenn Green Galleries; 45 (tr) George R.Nutter Fund, Courtesy, Museum of Fine Arts, Boston; 46 (t) Daniel J Cox/Tony Stone Images; 46 (b), 47 (t) The Putnam & Gosset Group; 47 (b) Ian G. Schoenherr; 48 The Metropolitan Museum of Art, Amelia B. Lazarus Fund, 1910. (10.228.7); 49 (t) Denver Art Museum,

Purchased with the funds from the National Endowment for the Arts Matching Fund and Alliance for Contemporary Art.; 50 © Wyland Studios, Inc.; 51 (t) Melissa W. Miller, "Northern Lights", Oil on Canvas, 66" x 74" 1982, Private Collection, Photo by Bill Kennedy; 52 Kunsthaus Zurich;

Unit 03:
Harcourt Brace & Company:
57 (b), 63, 65(b), 69(b), 71(b), & 73 Weronica Ankarorn;

Other: 54 National Academy of Design, New York City; 55 Eden Arts; 56 David Hockney, "Self Portrait With Folded Legs, Los Angeles, Sept 1982." Photographic Collage, 24 1/2" X 11 3/4", © David Hockey; 57 (t) Superstock; 58 Worchester Art Museum, Worchester, Massachusetts; 59 Samjai Fine Arts, Inc. 60-61 Reprinted with the permission of Simon & Schuster Books for Young Readers, an imprint of Simon & Schuster Children's Publishing Division from THE KEEPING QUILT by Patricia Polacco. Copyright © 1988 Patricia Polacco.; 62 Hunter Museum of American Art, Chattanooga, Tennessee, Gift of the Benwood Foundation/© 1998 Thomas Hart and Rita P. Benton Testamentary Trusts/Licensed by VAGA, New York, NY.; 64 Flag Day. (1935) Oil on canvas, 12 1/4 x 38 5/8" (31.1 x 98 cm). The Museum of Modern Art, New York. The Sidney and Harriet Janis Collection. Photograph © 1998 The Museum of Modern Art, New York; 65 (t) Private Collection; 66 Robert E. Daemmrich/Tony Stone Images; 67 (l) Picture Network International; 67 (r) Courtesy of the New York Public Library, The Branch Libraries, Picture Collection; 68 The University of Iowa Museum of Art, The Stanley Collection, X1990.656; 69 (t) Emily Rasky/Palo Alto Unified School District; 70 National Museum of the American Indian, Smithsonian Institution, #3384; 71 (t) Private Collection Switzerland; 72 Courtesy of Sharon Maczko;

Unit 04:
Harcourt Brace & Company:
77 (b), 79(b), 83(b), 89(b), 91(b), & 93 Weronica Ankarorn;

Other: 74 Courtesy of Inga Hunter; 75 Courtesy of Inga Hunter; 76 Jerry Jacka Photography; 77 (t) Philbrook Museum of Art Tulsa, OK.; 78 Los Angeles County Museum of Art, Gift of Max Palevsky and Jodie Evans; 79 (t) Scala/Art Resource; 80 (t) Table. (1944) Ebonized birch and glass, 15 5/8 x 36", The Museum of Modern Art, New York. Gift of Robert Gruen. Photograph © 1997 The Museum of Modern Art, New York.; 80 (b) "Paimio" Lounge Chair. 1931-33. Laminated birch, molded plywood, lacqured, 26 x 23 3/4 x 34 7/8". The Museum of Modern Art, New York. Gift of Edgar Kaufmann, Jr. Photograph ©1997 The Museum of Modern Art, New York.; 81 (t) "Red and Blue" Chair. (c. 1918), Wood, painted, 34 1/8 h. x 26" w. x 26 1/2" d., Seat height: 13", The Museum of Modern Art, New York. Gift of Philip Johnson. Photograph © 1997 The Museum of Modern Art, New York.; 81 (b) Tent (Star Gazer II). 1982, Nylon and aluminized nylon, 48" x 6' 8" x 7' 9" (122 x 203.2 x 236.2 cm) The Museum of Modern Art, New York. Gift of the designer. Photograph © 1997 The Museum of Modern Art, New York.; 82 The Museum Of Fine Arts, Houston, Gift of Miss Ima Hogg; 83 (tl) Everson Museum of Art,/Photography © Courtney Frisse.; 83 (tr) Instituto Nacional de Anthropolgia e Historia; 84 American Craft Council; 85 Elephant Chair with Lamp. (1928) Galvanized sheet steel, iron wire, lead, cloth, and painted-paper construction, 7 7/8 x 3 1/2 x 4 1/8" (19.7 x 8.9x 10.3 cm). The Museum of Modern Art, New York. Gift of the artist. Photograph © 1998 The Museum of Modern Art, New York., ©1997 Artists Rights Society (ARS), N.Y./ADAGP, Paris; 86-87 Eric Sander; 88, 89 (t) From the book MOLAS, Folk Art of the Cuna Indians, by Ann Parker and Avon Neal; 90 Ross Collection, Courtesy Museum of Fine Arts, Boston; 91 (t) Children's Art Exchange; 92 Armchair. 1964. Poured polyurethane, 29 1/2 x 44 1/4 x 35 1/4", Manufacturer: Executed at Dansk Polyether Industri, Denmark. The Museum of Modern Art, New York. Gift of the Designer. Photograph © 1998 The Museum of Modern Art, New York.;

Unit 05:
Harcourt Brace & Company:
97 (b), 99 (b), 103 (b), 105 (b), 111 (b), & 113 Weronica Ankarorn; 103 (t) Victoria Bowen; 106-107(c), 107 (br) Harcourt Brace & Co.;

Other: 94 Sotheby's New York; 95 UPI/Corbis-Bettmann; 96 (inset); 96 The Stock Market/G. Anderson; 97 (t) Tony Stone Images/Everett Johnson; 97 (c) The Stock Market/David Ball; 98 Tony Stone Images/Philip H.Coblentz; 99 (l) Scala/Art Resource, NY; 99 (r) Garry D. McMichael/Photo Researchers; 100, 101 Denver International Airport; 102 SuperStock/©1998 Jasper Johns/Licenced by VAGA, New York, NY; 103 (c) Photri, Inc.; 104 Courtesy of Emilio Aguirre; 105 (t) Metropolitan Museum Of Fine Art, New York City/SuperStock; 106(b), 107 (tr) & 107 (cr) Nawrocki Stock Photo; 106(c) & 107 (tl) Christina N. Mackenzie/Nawrocki Stock Photo; 108 Instituto Nacional de Anthropologia e

Historia, Mexico City; 109 Detail from Detroit Industry, south wall, by Diego Rivera. Photograph © 1996 The Detroit Institute of Arts, Gift of Edsel B. Ford; 110 Courtesy of Celia Alvarez Munoz; 111 (t) Courtesy of Monique Knowlton Gallery; 112 Viteri Center of Art, Quito, Ecuador;

Unit 06:
Harcourt Brace & Company:
117 (b), 119 (b), 123 (b), 125 (b), 129 (b), 131 (b), & 133 Weronica Ankarorn;

Other: 114 Collection of Mr. and Mrs. Richard Solomon, NY, The Pace Gallery; 115 Charles Moore/Black Star; 116 Courtesy Jean Albano Gallery; 117 (t) Musee Picasso, Paris. © Photo RMN-Beatrice Hatala, ©1997 Estate of Pablo Picasso, Paris/Artists Rights Society (ARS), N.Y.; 117 (c) David J. Getsy, 1988, "Experiment in Orange"; 118 The Metropolitan Museum of Art, Purchase, The Cape Branch Foundation and Lila Acheson Wallace Gifts, 1983. (1983.171); 119 (t) Courtesy of Frank Romero; 120-121 From Visual Merchandising and Display, 3rd edition. Written and photographed by Martin M. Pegler. Copyright © 1994 by Fairchild Publications, a division of ABC Media, Inc.; 122 (l) Courtesy of the artist; 122 (r) Art in America; 123 (t) Courtney Jasiulek, El Carmelo School/Palo Alto Unified School District; 124 Collection Walker Art Center, Minneapolis, Gift of Elizabeth McFadden, 1979; 125 (tl) Tom Wesselmann, "Porch", 1960. 9"x10", mixed media on board. (c)1998 Tom Wesselmann/Licensed by VAGA, New York, NY; 125 (tr) Object. (1936) Fur-covered cup, saucer and spoon; cup, 4 3/8" diameter; saucer, 9 3/8", spoon, 8" long; overall height 2 7/8". The Museum of Modern Art , New York. Purchase. Photograph © 1998 The Museum of Modern Art, New York.; 126 Detroit Free Press; 127 (tl), (tr), (br), (cr) Plymouth Ice Spectacular, Plymouth, MI; 128 The Stockhouse, Inc.; 129 (t) Romare Bearden, "Three Folk Musicians, 1967. 50 x 60", Collage on canvas one board (c)1998 Romare Bearden Foundation/Licensed by VAGA, New York, NY; 130 Colorado Springs Fine Arts Center; 131 (t) Georgia O'Keeffe, American, 1887-1986, Blue and Green Music, oil on canvas, 1919, 58.4 x 48.3 cm, Alfred Stieglitz Collection, gift of Georgia O'Keeffe, 1969.835, Photograph © 1996, The Art Institute of Chicago, All Rights Reserved, © 1996 The Georgia O'Keeffe Foundation/Artists Rights Society (ARS), N.Y.; 132 Philadelphia Museum of Art: The Louise and Walter Arensberg Collection;

Art Safety: 134-135 Harcourt Brace and Company/Terry Sinclair;

Exploring Art Techniques:
Harcourt Brace and Company: 141 (t) Sheri O'Neal; 148 (t) Sheri O'Neal; 156 (tr) Victoria Bowen; All others: Weonica Ankarorn;

Other: 137 (tl) © 1996 Marvy!/The Stock Market;

Elements and Principles of Design 152-153 (t) Damien Lovegrove/SPL/Photo Researchers; 152 (bl) Paul McCormick/The Image Bank; 152 (bc) Peggy & Ronald Barnett/The Stock Market; 152 (br) Gabe Palmer/The Stock Market; 153 (t) Harald Sund/The Image Bank; 153 (bl) John Gillmoure/The Stock Market; 153 (br) F. Tetefolle/Explorer/Photo Researchers; 153 (cr) Jim Corwin/Photo Researchers; 153 (cl) Will & Deni McIntyre/Photo Researchers; 154 (tl) Renee Lynn/Photo Researchers; 154 (tr) Nuridsany et Perennou/Photo Researchers; 154 (bl) Grafton Marshall Smith/The Stock Market; 154 (br) Tom Bean/The Stock Market; 154 (cl) Alan Carruthers/Photo Researchers; 154 (cr) Frank P. Rossotto/The Stock Market; 155 (c) Doug Plummer/Photo Researchers; 155 (tl) Stephen Marks/The Image Bank; 155 (tc) Charles D. Winters/Photo Researchers; 155 (tr) Lee F. Snyder/Photo Researchers; 155 (bl) Phil Jude/SPL/Photo Researchers; 155 (br) James Carmichael/The Image Bank; 156 (tl) Ed Bock/The Stock Market; 156 (tc) David Parker/SPL/Photo Researchers; 156 (br) Murray Alcosser/The Image Bank; 156 (cr) Chromosohm/Sohm/Photo Researchers;156 (cl) Adrienne Hart-Davis/SPL/Photo Researchers; 157 (c) Chris Collins/The Stock Market; 157 (tc) Arthur Beck/The Stock Market; 157 (tr) Raga/The Stock Market; 157 (bl) B. Seitz/Photo Researchers; 157 (br) Zefa Germany/The Stock Market; 158 (c) Brownie Harris/The Stock Market; 158 (tl) Michael Lustbader/Photo Researchers; 158 (tr) Alan & Linda Detrick/Photo Researchers;

158 (cl) Bryan F. Peterson/The Stock Market; 159 (tl) Stuart Dee/The Image Bank; 159 (tr) Patricio Robles Gil/Bruce Coleman, Inc.; 159 (bl) Sonya Jacobs/The Stock Market; 159 (bc) Bob Abraham/The Stock Market; 159 (br) David Sailors/The Stock Market; 159 (tcl) Wm. Whitehurst/The Stock Market; 160 (c) Michal Heron/The Stock Market; 160 (b) Aaron Rezny/The Stock Market; 160 (tl) Farely Lewis/Photo Researchers; 160 (tr) P. Saloutos/The Stock Market; 160 (bc) Jeff Hunter/The Image Bank; 160 (cl) Art Wolfe/Tony Stone Images; 160 (cr) Dan McCoy/The Stock Market; 161 (c) Charles Krebs/The Stock Market; 161 (tl) Zefa Germany/The Stock Market; 161 (tr) Bryan Peterson/The Stock Market; 161 (bl) Viviane Moos/The Stock Market; 161 (br) Jack Baker/The Image Bank; 162 (c) Art Stein/Photo Researchers; 162 (tl) Zefa Germany/The Stock Market; 162 (tr) Richard J. Green/Photo Researchers; 162 (bl) Dr. Jeremy Burgess/SPL/Photo Researchers; 162 (br) Joseph Nettis/Photo Researchers; 163 (t) Kevin Horan/Tony Stone Images; 163 (c) Geoff Dore/Tony Stone Images; 163 (bl) David Hall/Photo Researchers; 163 (bc) David Sailors/The Stock Market; 163 (br) Jeff Spielman/The Image Bank; 164 (c) Zefa Germany/The Stock Market; 164 (tl) Zefa Germany/The Stock Market; 164 (bl) Johnny Johnson/Animals Animals; 164 (br) Anup & Manoj Shah/Animals Animals; 165 (t) Kjell B. Sandved/Photo Researchers; 165 (tl) Will & Deni McIntyre/Photo Researchers; 165 (tr) Mickey Gibson/Animals Animals; 165 (bl) Russell D. Curtis/Photo Researchers; 165 (bc) Grafton Marshall Smith/The Stock Market;

Gallery of Artists (pg. 166-175) by artist's last name:
Aguirre, Courtesy of the artist; Bearden, Frank Stewart; Benton, Corbis-Bettmann; Bierstadt, National Portrait Gallery/Smithsonian; Biggers, Earlie Hudnall, Jr. ;Braque, Yousuf Karsh/Woodfin Camp & Associates, Inc.; Burchfield, PACH/Corbis-Bettmann; Calder, Inge Morath/Magnum Photos; Carr, City of Victoria Archives; Cassatt, National Portrait Gallery, Smithsonian Instituion /Art Resource, NY; Chagall, UPI/Corbis-Bettmann; Christo, © Christo, Photo by Sylvia Volz; Demuth, The National Gallery of Art Washington, DC, The Alfred Stieglitz Collection; Dove, Alfred Stieglitz/The Granger Collection, New York; Fish, Courtesy of Stewart & Stewart; Gauguin, Erich Lessing/Art Resource, NY; Hayden, Gift of the Harmon Foundation/Art Resource, NY; Hockney, Graham Finlayson/Woodfin Camp & Associates; Homer, Corbis-Bettmann; Hopper, PACH/Corbis-Bettmann; Hunter, Courtesy of the artist; John, Tate Gallery, London/Art Resource, NY; Johns, Dan Budnik/Woodfin Camp & Associates; Klee, Corbis Bettmann; Lawrence, Eden Arts; Maczko, Courtesy of the artist; Marin, Alfred Stieglitz/The Granger Collection, New York; Matisse, Cartier-Bresson/Magnum Photos; Miller, Bill Kennedy; Munoz, Courtesy of the artist; Nevelson, Charles Moore/Black Star; O'Keeffe, Dennis Brack/Black Star; O'Kelley, Little Brown and Company; Oppenheim, Courtesy of Independent Curators Incorporated(ICI), New York. Photograph by Nanda Lafranco.; Parker, Courtesy Ann Parker; Picasso, Giraudon/Art Resource, NY, © Estate of Pablo Picasso/Artists Rights Society (ARS), N.Y.; Polacco, Harcourt Brace & Co. ;Rivera, UPI/Corbis-Bettmann; Romero, Robert Berman Gallery; Ryan,Joan T. Washburn Gallery; Saar,Tracey Saar, Courtesy of Michael Rosenfeld Gallery, NY; Schoenherr, Ian G. Schoenherr; Searles, Courtesy of the artist; Thinh, Courtesy of Truong Thi Thinh; Tobey, Seattle Art Museum; Van Allsburg, Constance Brown; Van Gogh, Erich Lessing/Art Resource, NY; Viteri, The Viteri Art Center; Wesselman, Thomas Hoepker/Magnum Photos; Wharton, Courtesy of Margaret Wharton; Woodman, Courtesy Max Protech Gallery; Wyland, Wyland Galleries; Yani, © 1991 Byron Preiss Visual Publications, Inc. and New China Pictures Company, Photograph by Zheng Zhensun; Yazzie, Courtesy of the artist

Glossary:
176 (l) Doug Armand/Tony Stone Images; 176 (r) Peter Beck/The Stock Market; 177 (l) Robert Frerck/Odyssey; 177 (r) Robert Rathe/Stock, Boston; 178 Henley and Savage/Tony Stone Images; 179 Weronica Ankarorn/Harcourt Brace and Company; 180 (tl) Frank Siteman/Stock, Boston; 180 (tr) David Weintraub/Stock, Boston; 180 (bl) From the book MOLAS, Folk Art of the Cuna Indians, by Ann Parker and Avon Neal; 180 (br) Richard Blake/Tony Stone Images; 182 Courtesy of the National Museum of the American Indian, Smithsonian Institution, 23/3105; 184 Bob Daemmrich/Stock Boston;